Gosport *Then and Now*

Postcards from Gosport...and a few from Portsmouth

Gosport *Then and Now*

Postcards from Gosport...and a few from Portsmouth

PHIL HEWITT

First published in Great Britain in 2009 by
The Breedon Books Publishing Company Limited
Breedon House, 3 The Parker Centre,
Derby, DE21 4SZ.

This paperback edition published in Great Britain in 2014 by DB Publishing,
an imprint of JMD Media Ltd

ISBN 978-1-78091-390-2

Printed and bound in the UK by Copytech (UK) Ltd Peterborough

Contents

Introduction

There is something irresistible about the legend of the 12th-century Bishop of Winchester, who was shipwrecked off the south coast of Hampshire in a terrible storm. The story goes that local fishermen helped bring Henry of Blois ashore, at which point he tumbled to his knees on the beach and declared 'truly, this must be God's Port' – and so Gosport got its name.

The more prosaically-minded will claim that the name Gosport is a contraction of 'goose port' or 'gorse port', but I know which story I prefer. The colourful tale of Bishop Henry's grateful thanks for his safe deliverance is a much more appropriate prelude to the 900 years of rich and varied history which have followed.

When you think about it, much of Gosport's history seems just as unlikely as the good bishop's words. But while these words are rooted in myth, Gosport's development down the centuries is rooted in fact.

Who would have thought that a quiet fishing village would grow into the bustling home of a vast array of naval and military services? And yet it did, developing as a town ringed by forts as a first-line defence against a dastardly French invasion which never happened.

For a brief moment, the mighty dockyard which grew up in Portsmouth could have been relocated to Gosport. It was not, but the decision did not hold back Gosport's growth.

The ancient village of Alverstoke, where Gosport began, remained a village, but the town end expanded rapidly, becoming densely packed behind its ramparts. The admirals moved into Alverstoke, but in Gosport the pressgangs roamed, cholera raged and scores of pubs made it a decidedly lively place to be.

The naval and military services grew, barracks were built, a massive naval hospital was constructed, the railway arrived and stations proliferated. The huge workforce in Portsmouth dockyard brought a population explosion to Gosport, and by the time World War Two dawned, the town was more than ready to play a key role in the defence of the entire nation – a defence for which it paid a deadly price. More than a hundred civilians were killed by German bombs; more than half the town's houses were damaged.

In this book, I explore Gosport's fascinating history, using as my starting point my father Graham's collection of Gosport postcards – a collection he began in 1952, when he was a 13-year-old newspaper boy delivering papers to Park Road. Feeling sorry for an elderly couple who ran a shop from the front room of their cottage, he decided to help out by buying a few old postcards. The shop has long since gone, but the collection has grown in the half century since. Numbering several hundred, they offer a delightful insight into a Gosport which has disappeared.

I have chosen around 70 of the cards and then attempted to replicate them, standing as close as possible to where the original photographer once stood. Put the images together and you begin to see the many ways in which Gosport has changed as the times have changed around it. Combining fact, a little folklore and the odd personal reminiscence, I have used the postcards and their modern-day equivalents to tell the story of the town in which I grew up.

This book offers a journey around Gosport, beginning in the oldest part, Alverstoke, before visiting Stokes Bay and the site of the failed spa of Angleseyville. Our route continues through Haslar to pass over Haslar Bridge for a visit to the Ferry Gardens and a glimpse of Portsmouth. The images then take us along Gosport High Street and into Stoke Road and Bury Road before moving on to Lee-on-the-Solent for a look at its optimistic early years and its rather more controversial recent history. We then visit some of Gosport's churches before catching the ferry to Portsmouth for a final chapter looking at the city which has shaped so much of Gosport's history.

And so, let the tour begin...

Phil Hewitt
October 2009

1. Alverstoke

Gosport's Ancient Heart

It was Alwarestoch or Halwarestoke from the 11th to the 13th century, Alvardestoke in the 14th and Aillewardstoke in the 15th. For the past 500 years it has been Alverstoke. But whatever its name, Alverstoke has always been the ancient heart of the now sprawling borough of Gosport.

Bounded by water on three sides and yet nowhere facing the open sea, Gosport expanded massively northwards towards Fareham in the years following the Second World War. But it was in Alverstoke that it all began.

Dating back to Saxon times, the hamlet of Alverstoke is first mentioned under the name Stoke in a charter dated AD 948. A century later it was mentioned in the *Domesday Book*.

In the thousand years since, Alverstoke has been dwarfed by its upstart neighbour Gosport, subsumed into a borough boasting a population of 76,415 according to the 2001 Census.

Well into the 20th century, many people living in Alverstoke objected to the insertion of the word Gosport between the words Alverstoke and Hampshire in their postal address. Alverstoke was Alverstoke, and Alverstoke, they felt, was enough.

Alverstoke village centre in the first decade of the 20th century.

The buildings remain substantially unaltered a century later.

Today, Alverstoke continues to go its own way, taking pride in the fact that for most people it is, and always will be, simply 'the village' – an attractive, unspoilt alternative to Gosport's bustling town centre just over a mile away.

The postcard on the previous page, posted in the 1910s, captures much of the charm which Alverstoke still preserves today. To the right is The Five Bells public house, which closed in 1922 and is now a barbers' shop. Next door, in my boyhood, was a newsagent, a frequent stopping place for sweets on my way to Bay House School.

The more recent of the two photographs (above) shows the replacement tree for the earlier one that sadly died and which – even more sadly – probably was not the hanging tree we believed it to be on that trek to school 30 years ago.

Behind it today is the village fish and chip shop, an amenity which provoked considerable consternation among the Alverstoke die-hards when it first opened. Contrary to their predictions, however, Alverstoke has continued to flourish despite its presence.

Thoughts Of Quieter Times

Coming into view in the older photograph opposite is St Mary's Church, the centrepiece of the village of Alverstoke and very much a landmark on the Gosport skyline. More recent buildings obscure it in the present-day image, but there is still a reassuring continuity between the two photographs. Cars are parked where children once wandered, but, in this view at least, Alverstoke has changed remarkably little down the years. It is still a picturesque village grouped around its church.

Children walk the streets undisturbed by traffic in this 1910 postcard of Alverstoke.

A century later, new buildings obscure the church and cars clutter the streets.

The view shows Church Road leading off to the right towards St Mary's. On the left is Village Road, and here the buildings are substantially unaltered by the intervening decades. Harper & Co hairdressers now occupies 24 Village Road, the premises ostentatiously labelled Hope House in the earlier image, home then to Houghton's Boot and Shoe Shop. To its left, out of shot, was the post and telegraph office, run in the 1930s by the village stationer, Mrs Theresa Freeman. The service continues to this day.

Next door to the post office was Lloyds Bank. In the 1930s other businesses in Village Road included a dressmaker, a music teacher, an insurance agent, nurserymen, a grocer, a hairdresser and a beer retailer – all part of a self-sufficiency which Alverstoke has largely retained to this day.

Instant Answers

A century ago, there would have been three postal deliveries a day, and by all accounts they were highly reliable – a fact which meant postcards were used rather like a phone call or text message is today.

Posted to F.W. Hayes, HMS *King Edward*, Portland, on 6 April 1910, this particular card with its view of Village Road (below) has an appealing immediacy in the words on the back: 'Dear Fred, I have seen B. Redd and he tells me that you are at Portland. I shall be up at Fareham at 5 o'clock to meet you. Do not tell G.C. that you are coming. Your old chum, Fred.'

The postcard on page 9 of the children outside The Five Bells public house combines immediacy with brevity. Posted in 190? (the fourth digit is indecipherable), it was sent to Miss

An appealing image of Village Road in Edwardian times.

Again, the buildings stand largely unchanged 100 years later.

Hayes, near Frome, Somersetshire. The message reads: 'Did you receive my postcard about train inquiry at the station, love from Mother.'

Similarly interesting is the message on the back of a postcard of Green Lane sent on 4 August 1911 in confident expectation of its arrival that same day. Its recipient was Mr C. Lush, of Forton. The message ran: 'Could you come out to-night at 8 o'clock as I am going down to Lee. [Signature indecipherable].'

Rather chattier, 40 years later, is a postcard of St Mary's Church my father sent, on 4 July 1952, to his parents Mr and Mrs Hewitt, c/o Mrs Tuthill, Southend On Sea, Essex. Home was 43 Sydney Road, but in his parents' absence my father was staying with his Aunt Nance in Bridgemary, a couple of miles away.

'Dear Mum and Dad, I have come home in the dinner time. I am having a good time at Aunt Nance's and I hope you have a good time and the rain stops pourring [sic]. It poured continually all day yesterday and it was jolly cold. The exams have been jolly awful, but I'm getting on OK. Auntie Eve says that Tim had three saucers of milk and he jumped over the wall like a two-year-old this morning. I will write again Monday. Your loving son Graham.'

An interesting link between the two images here is the fact that the post office on the right is still the post office now.

A Fashionable Place To Live

Alverstoke again seems largely unchanged in this image of Village Road slightly further to the west, dating from around 1909 and showing children smartly dressed outside Mr Wilkins' corner store. The shop is now an off-licence. Again there is a pleasing absence of cars in the earlier image.

Children pose for the camera in front of the corner store a century ago.

By the time the photograph was taken, Alverstoke was very much the fashionable place to live and was distinctly residential in character. Alverstoke retained its rural charms well into the 19th century, which ensured a degree of tranquillity for the retired naval officers who started to flock to the district.

Kelly's Directory Of Gosport, Alverstoke, Fareham And District 1932–33 certainly gives an idea of the place it had become. It tells us that in this short stretch of road lived two rear-admirals, two

The children have gone, the cars have arrived and the corner store has become an off-licence, but otherwise little has changed.

commanders, a lieutenant-commander and a Royal Navy captain – a reflection of the fact that Gosport was by now very much a naval town. Gosport became an important ancillary to Portsmouth in the 1800s, a century which saw Britannia rule the waves. The town's naval role continued strongly into the 20th century.

Many of the men who tragically lost their lives during the sea battle of Jutland in 1916 lived in the Gosport area, and during the Second World War Gosport played a crucial role as host to a wide range of different naval services. By which time Alverstoke was very much the quiet backwater. It is strange, then, to reflect that the village so nearly lent its name to the entire borough.

Alverstoke claimed its right of historical precedence when it came to naming the successor authority to the Alverstoke Local Board in 1894, but the very much more populous town of Gosport challenged Alverstoke with its weight of numbers. The Alverstocracy wanted recognition of the fact that Alverstoke was founded first, but the Gosportians wanted the new Urban District Council to be named after Gosport. A compromise was eventually reached with the new designation, the Gosport and Alverstoke UDC.

Curiously, the battle was fought again a generation later. This time, however, Alverstoke was forced to give way. When borough status was secured in 1922, Alverstoke lost its place in the local authority's title, and Gosport Borough Council was born.

'Where We Got Married'

Looking grand in this 1930s image is St Mary's Church, dominating a still largely rural landscape. Much of the greenery survives today, although the area is less open.

This postcard was sent by Annie in 1936 with a suitably consoling message to Mrs E. Pearson, temporarily residing in Ward 10, Queens Hospital, Birmingham. 'Dear Lizzie. Hope you will soon be well again. Just look on the bright side. I bet you find it warm. Anyway we do. Just a card of the church where we got married. Hope you like it. We had a grand time as you might guess. Love Annie.'

Just 50 years before, Alverstoke would have been separated by fields from Gosport to the east, but as development gathered pace, so the parish of Alverstoke was forced to shed some of its outlying areas, with a number of separate parishes coming into existence between 1840 and 1913.

Another card, showing a similar image of the church but dated 1906, hints at the changes to the area. Written to Miss W. Sanderson, in Shanklin on the Isle of Wight, it was sent by 'your Freddie' to confirm his safe arrival in Gosport, seemingly prior to taking up employment in the dockyard.

'Lodgings fine, my sweetheart,' he tells her. 'Remembering the happy times we had here, sitting by the church. Was it really a year ago? Do you remember it, my sweetheart. Will be thinking such

Happy memories are recalled on the back of this 1930s postcard of St Mary's Church, Alverstoke.

St Mary's Church dominates the Alverstoke skyline.

grand and happy thoughts tomorrow. Remember walking through the fields? Will pass that way tomorrow on [my] way to work. We start at 8 in the morning. Other side of the harbour. I wish we had the time to do it last year. Perhaps this year. Sweet dreams, your Freddie.'

Educating The Children

Posted on 2 October 1905 to a Miss Riley, of Sheffield, the postcard (on page 19) carries the simple message – 'best love' followed by a signature presumably decipherable to the recipient.

The card tells us that this is School Lane, and there is a representative pupil just to prove it. But the name was never official. The proper designation was then, as it is now, Green Lane. Then, as now, it was impassable to road traffic.

Just a couple of hundred yards from St Mary's Church, Green Lane runs from Anglesey Road to Bury Road, an important link between two distinct parts of town.

Today, as you stand at this southern end of Green Lane, Alverstoke Junior School is out of view on the left, a few hundred yards further from the main road. In 1905, it was on the right-hand side where it had stood since 1842 when it was established as a National School, a product of early Victorian enlightenment.

National schools were created in 19th-century England and Wales by the National Society for Promoting Religious Education. In accordance with the teaching of the Church of England, these schools provided elementary education to the children of the poor.

Alverstoke School is on the right in this 1905 postcard.

Today houses occupy the site where the school once stood.

They were the major element in what was effectively the first near-universal system of elementary education in England and Wales. In the end, they were absorbed into the state system, either as fully state-run schools or as faith schools funded by the state.

The stated aim of the National Society was to set up a national school in every parish of England and Wales, usually next to or near the parish church and named after it, and it was as part of this movement that Alverstoke gained its school.

Built at a cost of £733, it had an initial attendance of some 200 of all age groups and enjoyed the advantages of being in what was generally regarded as the nicer part of town. Outbreaks of smallpox and other ailments in other areas made Alverstoke the preferred place for parents to send their children.

It was demolished in 1971 after nearly 130 years of service. Houses now stand on the roughly-triangular plot it once occupied. The large tree on the right has gone; road signs, rather than bollards, ban the traffic; and the newer, rather more functional streetlights make it all look rather drabber than it did a century ago.

Foster Gardens

Situated on the corner of Foster Road and Anglesey Road, Foster Gardens offer a mix of quietness and beauty which makes them a magnet for wedding parties looking for attractive backdrops to their souvenir photographs. On Saturdays in the spring and summer, the next group often arrives before the first group has finished – a tribute to one of Gosport's loveliest gardens.

Foster Gardens enjoy a much more open aspect from the road than they used to. The planting around the perimeter has recently been considerably thinned – and for good reason. The openness

My father sent this postcard of Foster Gardens to his parents in 1952.

Today, Foster Gardens are a popular spot for wedding photography.

allows you to look in and admire, but more importantly it is there as a disincentive to the antisocial behaviour which used to persist in the area. The older, denser bushes had provided cover of an altogether undesirable kind.

Fortunately things are rather brighter now for the park, which used to rejoice in the name King's Bottom until it was generally agreed that this could be misconstrued as an insult to the monarch.

In the garden itself, little has changed since it was first laid out. It remains a sheltered spot which lends itself well to the formal planting the local authority has brought to it, all designed around the central pergola, seating areas and pond.

The Borough Council's planting scheme consists of many Mediterranean plants and plants from California, New Zealand and other warm, dry countries, creating an exotic appearance that complements the existing trees, which include a magnificent weeping willow.

This particular postcard is another sent by my father to his parents in Southend-on-Sea in the summer of 1952. He was 13 at the time. He wrote: 'Dear Mum, I am writing on Sunday morning. It is a lovely sunny day and it is very warm. Yesterday Uncle Arch and the girls and I went to Lee [on-the-Solent] via Peel Common, Stubbington. We had a paddle in the sea. We walked the way. This afternoon we are going to the bay on the broken bus. It poured all Saturday night. Love from us all, love Graham.'

'The broken bus' was the local name for the open-top bus.

2. Stokes Bay, Little Anglesey and Haslar

Seaside Pleasures

Much as they do today, locals and visitors alike are enjoying the promenade at Stokes Bay in this older photograph (below), probably dating from the 1920s.

With its sweeping line of trees, Stokes Bay is one of the finest bays in the south, and it benefits from the fact that the developers have never been given the chance to take over. The promenade is well established, but Gosport has escaped the ghastly additions that so many other seaside stretches have had forced upon them.

The obvious attractions of Stokes Bay were formally recognised in the 1920s when the continuous walkway was built. Central government grants contributed, allowing the construction of refreshment rooms, public toilets and changing facilities.

The pavilion seen in the earlier photograph was demolished in 1989 and replaced with today's more modern structure, but the facilities have generally been on the minimal side of sufficient, enabling the bay to retain its unspoilt character. In fact, it is arguably less developed now than it used to be, for here stood Stokes Bay Pier, the remains of which were visible off-shore for many years – an attraction to the more adventurous swimmers despite the dangers.

With the creation of the promenade in the 1920s, Stokes Bay became a fashionable place to stroll.

Today the area to the right has been set aside for pétanque, in recognition of Gosport's long-standing twinning with the French town of Royan.

The pier – clearly discernible in the older picture – provided berthing facilities for the Isle of Wight steamers and was served by rail until the Stokes Bay line closed in 1915.

While it lasted, the pier, dating from 1842, was much vaunted for its panoramic views, embracing Southsea and the entrance to Portsmouth Harbour to the east; Southampton Water and the New Forest to the west; and the Isle of Wight from Bembridge to Cowes straight ahead.

Since then, the New Forest skyline has gained a significant new landmark, Fawley oil refinery. The largest facility of its kind in the UK, it was opened in 1921 by the Atlantic Gulf and West Indies Company. It is currently owned by Esso who acquired the site in 1925.

Preparing To Invade

In the 1848 *Topographical Dictionary of England*, Stokes Bay – 'to the south-west of Gosport' and in a sense still distinct from it – was described as 'justly celebrated for the excellence of its anchorage, affording security to an unlimited number of vessels.'

The Dictionary paints a vivid picture: 'On the shore forming this bay, and immediately opposite the fashionable town of Ryde, in the Isle of Wight, many good and handsome houses, besides an hotel, reading rooms and baths, have been erected within the last few years, and denominated Angleseyville.'

It is an arresting image of seaside elegance, but Stokes Bay's finest hour was not to come for another hundred years – D-Day.

The pleasing sweep of Stokes Bay has always been a key part of its attraction.

The blitzes of 1941 inflicted considerable damage on Gosport, but three years later the town, which had been on the front line throughout the war, went from the defensive to the offensive. In the spring of 1944, the whole area was in the grip of intensive preparations for D-Day, the Allied invasion of northern France.

Not a grain of sand in sight, but Stokes Bay still has plenty to recommend it – not least the fact that it remains largely undeveloped.

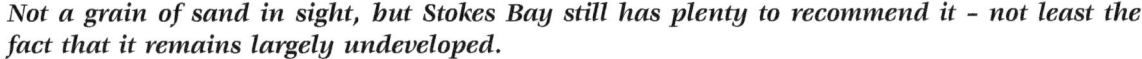

Gosport was one of the major embarkation centres for the sea-borne assault which marked the beginning of the end of the war in Europe. Stokes Bay, Lee-on-the-Solent, Hardway and Gosport town all played their part in the monumental operation. My father, born in 1939, counts among his earliest memories the tanks lining up nose to tail along Military Road as they awaited the greatest sea-borne invasion the world has ever seen.

As D-Day approached, the town was visited by the King, Prime Minister Winston Churchill and Field Marshal Montgomery. On the Bay itself, a solid two-storey building was constructed to control operations. The building is now home to Stokes Bay Sailing Club which was formed in 1938.

Stokes Bay was also one of the key sites for the testing and construction of the Mulberry Harbours which played such a crucial role in the landings, freeing the Allies from reliance on established ports by enabling them to take their own ports with them.

Nearby, the Royal Navy Armament Depot at Priddy's Hard supplied the armaments and the Royal Clarence Victualling Yard kept the troops fed. Later, Hardway saw the return of the wounded and prisoners. Gosport was truly at the heart of the war effort.

Mastery Of The Skies

In the foreground in these images is the shingle which is so characteristic of Stokes Bay.

In fact, the bay is part of the longest continuous shingle beach in England – a distinction some people might happily swap for just a little bit more sand in amongst all the stones.

Refreshments are offered 1920s-style in this postcard of the bathing station and café.

Rather more appealing are the current facilities along Stokes Bay.

But the lack of sand has not prevented Stokes Bay from emerging as an important centre for all manner of water sports. Just about any time of year, you can see people windsurfing, body-boarding, sailing or simply swimming. One of the great Gosport traditions is the New Year's Day dip in the bay's icy waters – a tradition which has raised thousands of pounds over the years for charity.

In the 1930s, at a time when Gosport was trying to promote the bay as a leisure attraction with its newly-completed promenade, Stokes Bay also became a focus for the mastery of the skies. The Coupe d'Aviation Maritime Jacques Schneider – better known as the Schneider Trophy – was a prize competition for seaplanes set up by the aircraft enthusiast Jacques Schneider in 1911. The idea was to encourage technical advances in civil aviation, but in reality it became a race for speed with laps over a triangular course.

Offering a prize of roughly £1,000, the race was held 11 times between 1913 and 1931, and in 1929 it came to Britain. As holders, the British decided that the 1929 Schneider Trophy would be competed from the Isle of Wight, with a four-sided 50km lap starting and finishing off Ryde Pier.

Huge crowds assembled on both sides of the Solent, with thousands flocking to Stokes Bay in particular.

And it was on the Stokes Bay shingle that thousands celebrated when the British won again, Supermarine racing to glory in the Supermarine S.6 at an average speed of nearly 330mph.

'One Of The Most Glorious Buildings In England'

I thought that everyone loved their school until I got to university and discovered that I was in a minority of one. But then again, not everyone had the privilege to go to Bay House School – a thriving comprehensive with a setting to die for.

The wooded, secluded country house which became the thriving Bay House School.

With park and woodland on three sides, it is built around a country house steeped in history, looking across Stokes Bay to the Isle of Wight. When Sir John Wolfenden opened new school buildings on the site in 1958, he declared it to be 'one of the most glorious buildings in England.'

Until 1972, this was Gosport County Grammar School. Before that, the main building – to which others have been added as the school has expanded – was variously a naval college, a private residence (home to Francis Sloane-Stanley) and, during the war, a base for the Royal Engineers.

Soon after the war, it became a satellite to the school which had grown up on the site of Gosport's Public Library and Technical Institute. Opened in the High Street in 1901, the Technical Institute grew rapidly. By 1921 it had a staff of 22 and, increasingly, space was a problem. Classes were held at the former St Matthew's School and Clarence School, and from September 1949 Bay House was also brought into service.

My father was part of the transition, starting at the High Street site in 1950 and then moving to Bay House in 1952 as more and more pupils moved across.

It was the first time he had been inside a genuine country house, he recalls. Not only were the grounds walled, but when he first went there they were also wooded at the front where the car park now stands. Inside the building were a number of white marble statues. The building was entering a new era, but it strongly maintained its country house aura.

Bay House School enjoys one of the finest settings of any school in the country.

It had been an enlightened decision to site the school in Bay House, and in headmaster Alan Walker, the school had exactly the right man to drive the school forward. He was never detached nor remote, my father recalls. Headmaster from 1937 to 1969, he was the most visible of heads, always available, the perfect man to oversee the school's expansion.

On 1 September 1972 Gosport County Grammar School amalgamated with Privett County Secondary School in order to provide for comprehensive education and is now known as Bay House School.

One Man's Vision

The Crescent, with its magnificent sweep, is one of Gosport's great landmarks, evoking comparison with its grander namesake in Bath.

Built in the late 1820s, it was at the heart of the resort known as Angleseyville – the brainchild of the visionary Robert Cruikshank who attempted to capitalise on the area's great potential.

Kelly's Post Office Directory for 1855 waxes lyrical about the charms of the resort Cruikshank created, lauding 'this beautiful village of modern date commanding extensive views of the Isle of Wight, Spithead and the Motherbank, the first stone having been laid by the Marquis of Anglesey in the year 1826.

'The situation is very elevated and the surrounding scenery commands universal admiration for its beauty and great variety, and in summer months it is much frequented by gentry for the benefit of its sea bathing and the beauties of its scenery.'

The milk arrives by horse and cart in this turn-of-the-century image of The Crescent.

Leafy and attractive, The Crescent remains one of Gosport's architectural gems.

These days it does not really exist in any practical sense as a separate entity. It is simply part of Alverstoke, but as late as the 1930s, Kelly's was listing it 'as a village and chapelry in the parish and union of Alverstoke, one mile south from Gosport Road station and two miles south from Gosport Terminal station, both on the Southern Railway (Western section).'

Sadly, the resort did not really take off, but The Crescent is its cherished legacy – 'a piece of grand urban planning of the early 19th century...unsurpassed in Hampshire', according to Pevsner (1967).

Thomas Ellis Owen was Cruikshank's architect. Between 1827 and 1831, he designed The Crescent, its flanking villas and nearby St Marks Road, where a pumphouse was situated.

The development was never completed, but it proved popular nonetheless, particularly with senior naval officers. In the 1930s The Crescent boasted among its residents Admiral Sir Thomas Jerram, Surgeon Rear-Admiral Welch, Commander Edward Helby, Vice-Admiral Fawckner, Rear-Admiral Austin, Captain Bent and Lieutenant Martelli.

Looking Towards Alverstoke

A solitary pedestrian, a horse-drawn cart and various boats by the water's edge...this is the attractive scene which would have greeted railway passengers in the 19th century as they travelled towards Gosport town centre from the coast at Stokes Bay.

As *The Pocket Guide To Gosport And Alverstoke* noted in 1911: 'The traveller who crosses the railway bridge over Stoke Lake on his way to Little Anglesey will see the Alverstoke Parish Church

This is the view rail passengers would have enjoyed on their way to Stokes Bay as the 20th century dawned.

Tower on the left and on making a closer acquaintance with the village will discover that many pleasant residences stand in the midst of pretty gardens.'

The railway bridge cut Stoke Lake – or Alver Creek as it is better known today – in two. This image (above) shows the western half, with the tower of St Mary's Church, Alverstoke, on the horizon to the left. Skirting it to the right is Little Anglesey Road.

The trains have long since disappeared, but the view towards Alverstoke remains.

Even here, we see the hand of Robert Cruickshank, founder of Angleseyville, the resort which nestled to the left between the creek and Stokes Bay. Cruickshank realised that the transport network would be key to the success of the spa which he envisaged. Consequently it was he who initiated the building of Haslar Bridge, connecting Angleseyville to the town centre at the harbour end of the creek, and it was he who promoted the branch railway line to Stokes Bay from which these views may be enjoyed.

Cruickshank even provided a church for his new resort. Despite opposition from St Mary's, he succeeded in establishing the Church of St Mark close to The Crescent. It was consecrated in 1844 as a Chapel of Ease to St Mary's – in other words, a church building other than the main church of the parish. It was demolished in 1911.

Pity The Poor Fellow

This much earlier image of Stoke Lake shows the water's edge before the creation of Little Anglesey Road. The banks are shored up with wood, and you can imagine it would not have taken much for the shoreline to become impassable.

Even now, the road is prone to flooding. It was a frequent complaint among friends with paper rounds during my boyhood that they simply could not get through in the worst of the winter flooding and had to take the long way round.

But with the lake's water intake controlled by the weir under the old railway bridge, the lake – albeit not a lake in the strictest sense – is generally regarded as safe for boating, much used by cubs and scouts and much fished in by local lads. It is also something of a hotspot for crabbers.

Passing along the edge of the creek must have been fairly hazardous before the road was created and the banks shored up.

The Shore, Little Anglesey.

The creek in the foreground makes this one of the most striking views of St Mary's Church.

This postcard of Little Anglesey (page 34) was sent on 30 July 1909 by Edith Fletcher to Miss E. White c/o Col Campbell, Eastney Barracks, Portsmouth, and the message on the back is a little gem.

'Dear E. Are you progressing quite well, I hope? I have been out all morning, nearly blowed away. Hope you got home safe Wed: I did enjoy myself, didn't you. That fellow is properly wet but we do not mind him taking us to the Kings [Theatre, Southsea] on Thurs!'

You just have to a feel a little sorry for the fellow, no matter how 'wet' he was.

The message becomes all the more interesting when you consider that the Kings was less than two years old at the time, having opened on 30 September 1907. It remains to this day one of the best examples of an elegant Edwardian playhouse in Britain, with many of its original features intact.

Crossing The Creek

It is much more overgrown now and these days it is a cycle track, but it does not require too big a leap of the imagination to see that the lower image overleaf was once part of Gosport's railway network.

The bridge was officially known as Little Anglesey Viaduct, but the popular name persists – Jackie Spencer Bridge. Spencer manned the bridge which replaced a ford across the creek.

The line itself was part of the expansion of Gosport's railway services in the mid-19th century. The railway reached Gosport in 1841, six years before it reached Portsmouth, and at its peak the town boasted eight passenger stations. One was situated on the pier at Stokes Bay, the culmination of the Stokes Bay branch line which passed across this bridge. The iron girders remain, but the line itself closed in 1915, after 52 years of service.

The Stokes Bay branch line, which closed in 1915, was an important part of the town's railway network.

Much of this particular line can still be followed on foot. Continue over this bridge and the former railway line will take you back towards the White Hart pub in Stoke Road, where the Gosport Road railway station once stood.

It is all rather greener and more overgrown now, but you can still see where the trains used to pass on their way to Stokes Bay. Gosport's disused railway lines are today an attractive walking route.

When the line closed, the route, it seems, could well have been opened up as a road for car traffic. After World War One, the line was bought by the local authorities with a view to creating a new access route to the bay, but the idea was shelved and eventually became redundant.

A gift of land by Mr G.V. Northcott in 1936 offered the chance to open up a better and wider route along what is now Jellicoe Avenue – an opportunity which was taken despite howls of complaint. 'Storm of protest over Gosport road scheme' ran *The Evening News* headline on 19 October 1937. The idea was dismissed as ridiculous, but the need to construct a road from Privett Road to Stokes Bay prevailed and the link was made.

During World War Two, Jellicoe Avenue was one of the bay approaches which served as an assembly point for vehicles waiting to embark after D-Day.

Gosport Park

Gosport is blessed with a wealth of open spaces. Towards the creek entrance and split in two by the South Relief Road is Walpole Park, one of the largest. Tucked behind the trees at the far end of Stokes Bay is Stanley Park, perhaps the most attractive.

Just as significant is Gosport Park, opposite Haslar Cemetery, on the other side of Haslar Creek. Created towards the end of the Victorian era, it is now a key location in Gosport's sports provision. With its six rugby pitches, Gosport Park is home to Gosport and Fareham Rugby Club. It is also home to Alverstoke Old English Bowling Club, cricket is played here too and there is a children's play area.

Gosport Park was created in the last years of the reign of Queen Victoria.

GOSPORT PARK.

Gosport Park remains to this day a centre for a number of sports or simply a pleasant place to stroll.

And the good news is that it will always remain an amenity. The park was originally common land known as Ewer Common, much used as a camping ground by gipsies, but under a provisional Order of the Lands Commissioners it was transferred to the Local Board in 1887 on condition that it was forever maintained as an open space.

It was unveiled to the public in 1891 and a fête was held to mark its opening.

The Evening News captured a flavour of the event: 'Wednesday was a red letter day in the history of Gosport. In magnificent weather, the new Park at Alverstoke was formally opened to the public. The afternoon was almost a general holiday, many of the tradesmen closing their establishments, from noon until seven o'clock. The whole town was *en fête* and never perhaps has anything excited more general interest than the opening of this fine piece of land. A piece of ground that was useless is now transformed into a well laid-out recreation ground.'

And so it remained. A pocket guide to Gosport in 1911 described it as 'a delightful resort, reached by the bridge over Workhouse Lake. The Park has an area of 30 acres, has broad paths shaded with trees and provided with comfortable seats. The cycle-track is considered one of the best in the southern counties, and the cricket pitches are kept in excellent order.'

Nearly a century later, it is still going strong, but the cycle-track has gone, with 'no cycling' signs now greeting you as you enter the park.

For more than 30 years, Haslar Cemetery was the burial ground for those who died in Haslar Hospital or on ships in Portsmouth Harbour.

Resting In Peace

Passing back over the former railway lines and continuing along Clayhall Road, you reach – after a few minutes' walk – Haslar Cemetery, a fascinating burial ground in which the dead really do rest in peace in the most attractive of leafy settings alongside the creek, facing Gosport Park.

For the first 70 years of its existence, the Royal Naval Hospital at Haslar provided its own burial site for those who died there or on ships in Portsmouth Harbour. But from 1826 to 1859, the role fell to the new Haslar Cemetery at Clayhall, home now to a number of important memorials.

Among the most interesting is the cemetery within a cemetery which contains the mortal remains of 26 sailors of the Turkish Navy whose ships had the misfortune to dock off Gosport in 1850 – misfortune because just a couple of years earlier hundreds of people had died in a cholera outbreak in the town. Mid-19th-century conditions in old Gosport town left a great deal to be desired.

Most of the crew of the Turkish ships contracted cholera during their stay and were treated at Haslar Hospital; a number died, and so did several others in training accidents while they were in the town. Originally buried in the grounds of Haslar Hospital, they were later exhumed and reburied in Haslar Cemetery.

Another key memorial is the Eurydice Memorial, a tribute to the hundreds of lads who lost their lives when the *Eurydice* training ship capsized off the Isle of Wight on 24 March 1878 in one of Britain's worst peace-time naval disasters. A 24-gun frigate, the *Eurydice* was caught in a heavy snowstorm and foundered. Only two of the ship's 364 crew and trainees survived. Reported sightings of a ghost ship have since ensured that the ship has entered naval folklore.

Many important memorials are to be found in Haslar Cemetery.

Also at Haslar Cemetery is the memorial to the men of the A1 submarine disaster. The Royal Navy's first British-designed submarine, the A1 sank on 18 March 1904 during a training exercise off the Isle of Wight when it collided with the steamer *Berwick Castle*. The water was only 12 metres deep, but the boat flooded and the entire crew – between 11 and 14 strong, depending on the account you read – were drowned.

Haslar Bridge: An Important Link

Continuing past Haslar Cemetery, you soon reach the mouth of Haslar Creek which is now crossed by a road bridge taking you into the old town of Gosport, today its main shopping area.

Just before you reach the bridge, you pass the former Royal Naval Hospital at Haslar – a major reason Haslar Bridge has been so important over the years.

Without the bridge at Haslar, anyone arriving in Gosport from Portsmouth faced a long detour through Alverstoke and Clayhall to reach the hospital, and this was the case throughout my childhood for all car traffic from the town.

A footbridge spanned the creek, passing over the remains of the old road bridge which had been all but destroyed during the war. It had been bombed and its centre span had been removed to enable ships to pass in for repairs. All that remained of the old bridge was a great place to sit and fish.

The fact that the old bridge's sides did not meet in the middle is probably the reason the Clayhall area escaped the intensity of post-war redevelopment seen elsewhere in the borough. It was effectively cut off.

Before there was a bridge at all, a little ferry carried passengers across, with heavy goods having to be taken by road. But in 1791 a grant was made to a Gosport merchant by the name of Forbes

Over the years various bridges have spanned the mouth of Haslar Creek at this point.

The present bridge dates from 1979 and is open to cars. Holy Trinity Church to the right is a familiar Gosport landmark.

for the 'liberty of building a bridge for which he is to have a certain toll and it being a considerable thoroughfare will be found more convenient than the usual mode of ferrying over.'

Forbes Bridge was the result, but it soon proved unsound. It was a shaky structure which deteriorated rapidly and quickly became too small for the volume of traffic anyway. A new toll bridge was built, thanks to the enterprising Robert Cruickshank who was keen to open up another route to his new spa at Angleseyville.

The tolls were dropped in 1879, when in view of the bridge's importance to the Navy, the Local Board suggested that the Admiralty should take it over and throw it open to the public free of charge. A penny charge was later reintroduced, but payment was very hit and miss depending on whether there was anyone there to collect the toll.

The post-war period saw the construction of the lofty footbridge, known to everyone as Pneumonia Bridge for obvious reasons. It got pretty cold up there.

Pneumonia Bridge on the left lived up to its name.

The present bridge dates from 1979, and to its right in the new picture (page 41) is the popular Haslar Marina, built in 1993 to cope with the large demand for marina berths in the Solent.

Providing continuity between the two images is the tower of Holy Trinity Church, once the highest point on the Gosport skyline view from Portsmouth. Post-war tower blocks now dwarf it.

'An Immense Pile Of A Building'

In these two images of Haslar Bridge, below and overleaf, it is viewed from the northern, town side of Haslar Creek – a good vantage point from which to consider the important naval role the area once enjoyed.

Haslar Creek was home to our coastal forces, and HMS Dolphin at the harbour entrance was home to the submarine service. In 1992, it was announced that the submarine fleet would be leaving HMS Dolphin and moving to HMNB (Her Majesty's Naval Base) Devonport.   The

Today crossing Haslar Creek is rather more civilised.

submarine school remained until 1999, but the last submarine left Dolphin in 1994. HMS Dolphin was formally decommissioned in 1998.

Elsewhere in the town were HMS Daedalus and HMS St Vincent. But perhaps the greatest of the town's naval establishments was the Royal Naval Hospital at Haslar. Its tower can be seen in both these images, but while the tower might still be there, the hospital is not – a loss Gosport is still coming to terms with.

Initially the hospital was built to tend to the navy, but it also served the army and the RAF and in more recent years many thousands of civilians. Sadly, however, and despite a massive fight to save it, Haslar Hospital was decommissioned in the summer of 2009, bringing to an end more than two and a half centuries of care.

Casualties from all the major wars were treated in Haslar Hospital, from Waterloo through to the Falklands War, from both World Wars, from Trafalgar and from the Crimean.

So great was the need, that Haslar was operational nine years before it was completed. It opened in 1753, taking 16 years in all to build. During its construction, chief physician Dr James Lind described the hospital as 'an immense pile of a building and when complete it will certainly be the biggest hospital in Europe!'

In December 1998 the Save Haslar Task Force was formed to fight its closure. Massive protests were held, the government was petitioned and the battle to save the hospital was thrashed out in the House of Commons. But all to no avail.

In 2001 the provision of acute healthcare within Royal Hospital Haslar, as it was by then known, was transferred from the Defence Secondary Care Agency to the NHS Trust. But in July 2009, the battle was finally lost.

The once bustling military hospital was reduced to an empty shell. The hospital was gutted of most of its equipment as services transferred to the new so-called superhospital eight miles away, Queen Alexandra at Cosham, and the 300 military doctors and nurses who worked on the site were relocated.

3. The Ferry

Gosport's Proud Naval Heritage

Passing over Haslar Bridge, you soon reach the Ferry Gardens. Here you can look across and see the presence which has arguably most influenced Gosport's development over the past 500 years: the city of Portsmouth.

Portsmouth occupies the eastern side of Portsmouth Harbour, Gosport the western side. Several hundred yards of water separate the two, but also join them inextricably.

In 1627, a survey of Portsmouth Dock questioned whether it would not be better to start a new dockyard on the Gosport side – an idea which never came to fruition. But in Portsmouth's shadow, Gosport developed significantly to become vital to the overall success of the harbour. Between them, Portsmouth and Gosport offered a great defence against the invader and a great base for the fleets with which Britain ruled the waves.

The fleets assembled from Portsmouth, but it was Gosport with its victualling station and wealth of storehouses, timber yards and rope-walks which supplied them. And with the great naval hospital at Haslar on the Gosport side of the harbour, it was to Gosport that the casualties returned.

All of which contributed to Gosport's rapid expansion. With little residential land close to the dockyard in Portsmouth, dockyard workers found it easier to seek accommodation in Gosport. My own grandfather did exactly that in the 1930s.

Gosport's proximity to Portsmouth – seen on the left here across the harbour – has long defined the town's character.

Portsmouth Harbour from Gosport

Passengers enjoy a degree of shelter from the elements as they board the Gosport ferry on the Gosport side for the short crossing to Portsmouth.

Inevitably, Gosport's fortunes, like Portsmouth's, were intimately linked to conflict. Put simply, when there was war, the harbour prospered. And with the long conflicts and threat of conflict with France during the 1700s and early 1800s, Gosport was transformed.

In just a hundred years, it went from being a small coastal fishing village to become, as the 19th century dawned, a substantial town; walled, moated and very much dependent on the navy.

Pressgangs were active in the town; French prisoners were held here; and the town grew significantly, quietening down only with the conclusion of the French Wars following Napoleon's final defeat at Waterloo on 18 June 1815.

Crossing The Harbour

Given Gosport's close relationship with Portsmouth, it was inevitable that an important challenge facing both communities was how best to cross the water between them.

A boy in a sailor suit is among the passengers waiting to cross to Portsmouth in this appealing image of the Gosport ferry.

The land route from Gosport was a long one, going through Fareham and Portchester and then all the way through Portsmouth. Just a few hundred yards in distance, the water route was the obvious one – but one often fraught with difficulties.

The view of Portsmouth from Gosport's Ferry Gardens is an impressive one. Portsmouth's Round Tower, part of the city's coastal defences, can be seen on the right.

The 1911 *Pocket Guide To Gosport*, a treasure trove of evocative description, does not let us down in the picture it paints of crossing the harbour: 'Gosport is seen to advantage as it is approached by water from Portsmouth, a panorama of rich and historic interest being presented. Immediately in the foreground is a good sprinkling of grimy long-shoremen and hale and weather-beaten salts like old sea-birds driven by stress of weather to the nearest land.'

It is an arresting image, and the writer becomes quite lyrical: 'The *tout ensemble* gives a most picturesque and unique effect that can scarcely be equalled for quaintness on the English coast.'

But the fact is that the ferry crossing was frequently a source of discord. As far back as 1602, the rights of the matter were being hammered out, with a court case determining just who owned the ferry. Was it Gosport at large or a particular group of boatmen?

The courts concluded that it simply was not safe 'that the ferry or sea passage should be under the rule and direction of any one man.' Instead, it decided that a Commission should be set up to control the ferry. But the battles continued, raging particularly in times of great naval activity when the ferrymen found themselves in an even greater position of power. Effectively they could hold their customers to ransom, especially as these customers were often sailors anxious to get to their ships and not simply across the harbour.

There are plenty of accounts of uncouth, exploitative ferrymen charging ludicrous fares during the Napoleonic Wars – a situation worsened by the fact that many of their craft were barely seaworthy anyway. The 19th century saw a number of attempts to force them to clean up their act and be reasonable in the prices they charged. But generally, the boatmen, with their superior knowledge of the harbour, were the ones who had the final say. The issue was settled with the outbreak of peace when Portsmouth and Gosport became quieter again.

The Bridge That Floated

It sounds rather fanciful now, but in the 1930s the idea of a railway tunnel under Portsmouth Harbour gathered a fair head of steam, advocated by the energetic Lew Hanbidge.

Mr Hanbidge, chairman of the Gosport Association, had met the inventor, was impressed by the scheme and felt a decent alternative to the ferry was long overdue.

It was said that the Kearney High Speed Tube would get you across the harbour in 50 seconds. With war clouds gathering, it was even touted as a possible air-raid shelter. Even the mayor suggested Gosport had been too patient in putting up with its 'ancient' ferry system.

The response from the traders was predictable. At a stroke the slogan 'Shop in Gosport' would be changed to 'Shop in Portsmouth', they said – a view which has persisted. Back in the 1970s, the argument used to run that if you provided easy vehicle access to Portsmouth across, under or over the harbour, you would kill Gosport commercially. The feeling was that a tunnel, a road bridge or a car ferry would be the death of the High Street, cutting a hole in Gosport through which all business would fatally flow.

It is a moot point. But these days with any such link no longer on the agenda, Gosport has adopted a rather sadder role – as a car park for the many thousands who want to shop the other side of the harbour.

Until half a century ago, you could take your car across to Portsmouth by the ferry known as the floating bridge.

Nothing remains of the floating bridge car ferry today, and few people would argue for the return of a car ferry service.

It is strange, then, to reflect that until comparatively recently, Gosport and Portsmouth did indeed have the car ferry link that so many have subsequently feared – albeit on a fairly modest scale. Portsea Island was linked with mainland Gosport in 1840 with the launch of the so-called floating bridge.

The 1911 *Pocket Guide to Gosport* tells of travel options unthinkable today. You could take your vehicle onto the floating bridge at Portsmouth, sail to Gosport, park in town, take the train to Stokes Bay Pier and thence sail to the Isle of Wight. A hundred years later, none of this is possible.

But the reference to the railway is significant, for Gosport's rail links made the floating bridge all the more important.

A ferry to take horses and light carriages across the harbour was built in 1834, and this in turn led to demands for a ferry capable of taking heavier vehicles over the water. Hence the floating bridge, which made its first crossing of the harbour on 11 May 1840. The link to the Isle of Wight followed in 1842. A pier was built at Stokes Bay and the Gosport railway line was connected to it.

Pulled on chains and capable of taking 20 cars at a time, the floating bridge operated between Gosport and Broad Street in Portsmouth until the service ceased in 1959.

Improving The Ferries

It is fair to say that the current ferry arrangement for foot passengers between Gosport and Portsmouth effectively dates back to Victorian times. A century and more ago, steam launches started from Gosport Hard at intervals of six minutes – more or less as the ferries do today. The service was complemented by the floating bridge which ferried vehicular traffic between the towns (Portsmouth did not become a city until 1926) every half hour.

The ferries have long been an important part of the traffic crossing Portsmouth Harbour.

The ferry pontoon is an ideal place from which to appreciate the perfect natural harbour which separates Portsmouth on the left and Gosport on the right.

In the years since, the ferries have been regularly updated to provide increased comfort. Children of the 1960s will remember the more primitive, open-air versions. I looked over the side of one once. My glasses slipped off my nose and for a split second were perched perilously half on the ferry, half on the pontoon. As the ferry slipped away, so my glasses slipped to the bottom of the harbour.

As times change, so too do fashions. Back in the 1970s, the ferry company proudly boasted a cruising boat for those more leisurely tours of the harbour, away from the endless routine to- and fro-ing of the passenger ferries. In a name which tried to capture its spirit of adventure as it launched into the harbour, the boat was named the *Gay Enterprise* – a name later changed for obvious reasons.

Other rather more significant changes include the creation of a proper pontoon with subsequent, periodic improvements. In Victorian days, the foreshore was slimy and dangerous. The need for a proper landing stage became pressing – a need recognised by the boatmen just as much as by the passengers.

In 1872, Parliament granted the Trustees permission to construct 'a wharf and pier or jetty at Gosport' with all necessary approaches and works. The Trustees were given the power to erect toll houses and landing stages and to dredge the harbour in the immediate area.

Things improved again in the early 20th century with the construction of a new wharf, a floating pontoon and a gangway – at a cost to the ratepayers of nearly £60,000.

An Attractive Place From Which To View The Harbour

The Ferry Gardens are the natural place from which to enjoy Gosport's view of the harbour and of Portsmouth opposite. Now renamed the Falkland Gardens, they date back to the 1920s when the old Hard area was filled in. Land was reclaimed to raise it above the tidal levels of Portsmouth Harbour and the whole area started to take on much the look it enjoys now, with its paths and fountain centrepiece.

The scheme was partly to provide labour for the unemployed, with the project being paid for through central government funding; but the end result was to enhance an area very much in need of attention.

Once a rough-cobbled Hard, prone to flooding and with coal barges a frequent sight, it has long since become a popular place to sit and relax. Judging by the photographs, my brother and I seem to have spent most of our childhood here. My mother worked nights as a nurse, and my father used the Ferry Gardens as a great place to air two rowdy young boys during the day at weekends.

Old postcards label the area the Esplanade Gardens, but initially they were known as Harvey's Promenade after a local councillor. Later they became the Ferry Gardens, the name by which most people still know them, though in 1984 Prime Minister Margaret Thatcher officially renamed them the Falkland Gardens to mark Gosport's key role in the Falklands War of 1982.

The Gardens also mark Gosport's long-standing friendship with the French town of Royan. Part of the Ferry Gardens was renamed the Royan Gardens in 1973 at a ceremony in which a tree of friendship was planted. Sadly the tree died within weeks, but the links between Gosport and its

Gosport's Ferry Gardens have long been a pleasant place to sit.

Across the harbour, the dockyard and HMS Victory *are points of continuity between this present-day image and its older equivalent.*

French twin are still flourishing. In May 2009, the walkway known for many years as the Esplanade and later as the Millennium Promenade was renamed the Esplanade de Royan in honour of the 50th anniversary of the Gosport-Royan twinning.

The Ferry Gardens consist of flower beds for traditional Victorian bedding schemes, two carpet beds redesigned each year to celebrate notable anniversaries, plus shrub beds and seating.

These days the Gardens are part of a wider development marking the new millennium. May 2000 saw the completion of a £3 million redesign of the entire esplanade area. The popular Gosport Waterfront Trail, a self-guided walk through approximately 3km of historic Gosport, is a great way to enjoy it.

The postcard on the previous page of his home town was sent to my father by his parents when he was an 18-year-old visiting a penfriend in Finland in 1957.

Approaching The High Street

You cannot help feeling that the older photograph (right) captures a rather more elegant age, from the soldiers and sailors on the left to the gentleman with the folded newspaper and stick on the right. The smartly-dressed mothers with their children on the bench and the beautiful street furniture seen here – perhaps in the 1920s – are part of an age which has gone. The charm is definitely lacking in the present-day image overleaf.

Turn your back to the ferry and Portsmouth Harbour, and this is the view – now and maybe 80 years ago – which you see as you move towards Gosport's principal shopping area, the High Street.

To the left, out of view, is Gosport's bus station – pretty much where Gosport's Parliamentarians set up their guns for the siege of Royalist Portsmouth during the English Civil War.

To the right in the older picture is Gosport's distinctive Market House which stood on the corner of the High Street. In the late 18th/early 19th century, an earlier Market Hall had stood in the

Arriving in Gosport 80 years ago must have been impressive indeed.

centre of the High Street – or Middle Street as it was then known – opposite The India Arms Hotel.

The building seen in the above photograph was severely damaged during an air raid in 1940 and was eventually pulled down in the 1960s. The cellars of the derelict Market House became the Dive Café where – so my father recalls – many would marvel at the sight of Mr Tomlinson pouring a dozen cups of tea in one go without stopping or spilling any.

Nearby, on the old Gosport Green near the harbour, the Gosport Fair was held twice a year on 4 May and 10 October. Towards the end of the 19th century, it was felt that the fairs had become a

The old-style lamps do not quite recapture the old-style elegance in this image of the approach to Gosport High Street, though the Ferry Gardens remain an attractive place to watch the world go by.

corrupting influence, and in 1896 the new Urban District Council began to call for their discontinuance. As the *Victoria County History* noted in 1908: 'The fairs had much deteriorated in the 19th century, when toys were the only articles sold in any quantity.' They were finally abolished in 1900.

4. Gosport High Street

'Handsome And Populous'

You can almost feel the character in this gorgeous 1914 image (below) of Gosport's High Street – a character rather lacking in its modern-day equivalent.

It is worth pausing to savour the period detail – the children about to cross the road on the right, the boys posing with a hoop on the tram tracks, the carts from Cookes Stores parked on the left, the pubs, the hairdressers, the obvious quietness of it all.

There is little to rival it in the recent picture, taken on a near-deserted Sunday afternoon but without the charm.

In both, this is the commercial heart of the town, and in the time of the earlier photograph it was also the most densely populated part of the town after Gosport's 18th-century growth spurt. Situated in the south-east of the district, between the inlets of Forton Lake and Haslar Lake, the town area developed rapidly – in sharp contrast to Alverstoke which as yet remained resolutely rural.

An 1801 guide to Gosport notes the attractions of the High Street, or Middle Street as it then was: 'The town itself is handsome and populous, the principal street is Middle Street, which is broad and well-built, extends westward from the harbour to the works and is of a great length, and were it not for the obstruction of the market place would be exceeded by few.'

There is a wealth of detail to savour in this 1914 image of Gosport High Street, which was clearly very different to the High Street we see today.

Gosport High Street on a sunny Sunday afternoon.

The *Victoria County History* in 1908 is somewhat less enthusiastic: 'The buildings are in no way remarkable; in High Street, which is the principal road, is a Market Hall built in 1812, and other public buildings are the free public library, opened 1901, and the Thorngate Memorial Hall, 1885, while in South Street is the Connaught Drill Hall, built in 1902.'

As so often, it is the 1911 pocket guide which is the most evocative – even if it does damn with slightly faint praise, describing the High Street as 'a thoroughfare paved with woodblocks and containing one or two notable buildings.'

I think we can afford to be a little bit more positive about our modern High Street. The shops might not be the most attractive that Hampshire has to offer, but look up and there is still much to enjoy in the High Street's mix of Georgian, Victorian, Edwardian and modern buildings.

A Fortified Town

Gosport's pedestrianisation looks pleasant enough in the recent image (below right), another summer Sunday afternoon, but the older picture should clinch it: Gosport lost far more than it gained with the advent of pedestrianisation nearly 20 years ago.

Gosport's pedestrianisation came at a time when many of our high streets were losing or had actually lost their individual character. Many will argue the opposite, but I cannot help feeling that pedestrianisation accelerated the process in Gosport's case.

However congested the High Street was when traffic went right through it, at least it bustled with life – which is not always the case now.

Horse-drawn transport was clearly still the order of the day in this archive image of Gosport High Street.

And if it seemed cramped, then perhaps we should remember that it was always in the nature of this part of Gosport that it was hemmed in, not least by its fortifications.

Ramparts were built around the town in the mid-1800s to protect it from possible attack from French invaders – an almost instinctive response in a century of French threat, real and imagined.

Look up, and it is clear that many attractive buildings have survived in Gosport High Street.

The belief, which reached a peak again in the mid-19th century, was that Gosport was the vulnerable point through which Portsmouth might be taken. If Gosport fell, the dockyard stood open, with potentially disastrous consequences for Britain's fighting fleet.

Inevitably, the ramparts not only kept out, but they also kept in, with little expansion happening beyond them. Consequently the town became congested. Gosport's population in 1821 was 10,342; 20 years later it was 13,510. By 1851 it was 16,908; 10 years later it was 22,653 – doubling in just 40 years, with the majority living increasingly cheek by jowl within the fortified area.

Not surprisingly, conditions, at various times and despite various attempts to improve them, verged on the appalling, with disease rife and accommodation frequently woeful. Worsening the situation was the influx of workers from the dockyard in Portsmouth. Life in Gosport might not have been wholesome, but it was certainly cheaper than life in Portsmouth.

By the late Victorian era, there was pressure for some kind of slum clearance programme – one which arguably was not fully realised until the German bombers did their worst during World War Two.

The Ale Flowed Freely

With density of population went ubiquity of watering holes. In centuries gone by, Gosport had a quite staggering number of public houses.

Some of the pubs were part of the communications network. Hyslop's horse omnibus departed from The India Arms in the High Street to meet trains arriving at the station. The Old Northumberland, pictured here in the older photograph, was a main posting house.

Many more, though, were simply places in which to drink.

The Old Northumberland was an important High Street pub.

GP 2   GOSPORT. HIGH STREET

The Old Northumberland pub has long since gone, replaced by rather nondescript shopping outlets.

In North Street alone in the mid-19th century there were The Rodney's Head, The Black Lion, The Lord Nelson, The Green Dragon, The Star & Garter, The Queen's Head, The Sun Tavern, The Waterman's Arms and The Red Lion – and that was not all of them.

South Street offered The George & Dragon, The Bunker's Hill, The Little Red Lion, The Princess Royal, The Rodney's Engagement and the quaintly-named Artichoke. Nearby Beach Street boasted, if boasted is the right word, The Bridge Tavern, The Phoenix, The Cross Keys, The Three Tuns, The Union, The Two Sawyers, The Hare & Hounds, The Navy Tavern and Dover Castle.

Add them all up and the High Street area offered something like 150 pubs as Queen Victoria entered her second decade on the throne – serving a population of more than 6,000 people crammed into the same square quarter mile within the old ramparts. Today there are just a handful of pubs in the area.

It is an era which, of all Gosport's historians, former Gosport Mayor Trevor Rogers evokes most colourfully. Writing for the Gosport Historic Records And Museums Society in 1973, he vividly puts the pubs in the wider context of the general street scene. During the Napoleonic Wars, as he says, it would have been a lively area indeed, home to soldiers, housewives, post-captains, warrant officers, boat builders, shopkeepers, attorneys and many crafts which have long since disappeared such as soapboilers, slop-fellers, muffin-men, block-makers and china-menders.

On top of that were the alehouses, three coach-houses, two theatres, a bridewell, three breweries, two flour mills, 14 bakehouses, an iron foundry, malthouses, warehouses and wharves. Busy indeed.

Shops Come And Go

It was in The India Arms public house that a significant number of meetings were held aimed at improving the area. In the mid-1700s there was a meeting to discuss how best to clean up the town, including the appointment of a nightwatchman; around the same time there was a meeting to discuss fundraising for the purchase of the Duke of Chandos' organ for Holy Trinity Church; and in the early 1800s the operation of the ferry was debated here.

In the older picture (previous pages), the High Street is looking considerably busier than it did in the images in the previous section. Poverty was still a significant problem in the interwar and immediate post-war years in Gosport, and behind these shops would have been plenty of unacceptable housing just ripe for demolition. On the surface at least, however, the town centre was clearly bustling, if not prosperous.

Just to the left of The India Arms was Woolworth's, one of the most mourned victims of the 2008–09 recession. Woolworth's went into administration in November 2008 with debts of £385m, Deloitte was unable to find a buyer and so the firm's 807 British stores launched their clearance sales, the start of a staged programme of closure that left more than 27,000 people unemployed. With those jobs went a piece of history, a part of all our childhoods.

One of the original American five-and-dime stores, the F.W. Woolworth Company was simply unbeatable in the early 1920s, at the forefront of a retail revolution that introduced good-quality

Many Gosport pubs have disappeared since the war. This stretch of the High Street was once home to The India Arms.

mass-produced goods that everyone could afford. Customers loved it, and the company expanded massively. The Gosport store was an important part of the High Street scene.

Other familiar 1930s High Street stores in Gosport included H.S. Masterman & Sons tailors, just to the right of The India Arms. Also nearby on this southern side of the High Street in the early 1930s were Freeman Hardy & Willis bootmakers; Webb stores, purveyors of fancy leather goods; F. Eager & Sons, pastrycooks and bakers; Meotti's Swiss Café; Boots Cash Chemists; and Gorman's grocers.

What Became Of Edward?

The women in their hats add an easy elegance to the photograph below, completed by the two smart gentlemen strolling down the tram tracks. Would it be disrespectful to suggest that there is something faintly reminiscent of Laurel and Hardy about these two fellows as they go about their business?

On the right of the modern view overleaf the 1960s Town Hall has changed things considerably; on the left, the buildings are remarkably unaltered.

Addressed to Mrs Gearing, of Camberwell, London, on 26 July 1912, this postcard was despatched from Matron's Quarters, R N Hospital, Haslar – with due concern for domestic detail.

'Dear Mrs Gearing. You see I am here safely. My luggage was here first this time. It is beautifully cool but sunny today. I believe I left a shilling on the shelf of the gas meter. Do you mind putting it in for me as I'm not sure what became of it. I hope the children on the steps have not quite driven you out of your minds yet. With kind regards to you all, yours sincerely J.B. Curtis.'

The western end of Gosport High Street is captured in this appealing image, a postcard sent in 1912.

The ubiquitous closed-circuit television camera surveys an empty High Street in this present-day image. Gosport's Town Hall is on the right.

Another interesting inscription, though sadly undated, is on the back of a postcard of the Public Library and Technical Institute featured opposite:

'Dear Lill, I'm a bit late to send you your answer for I was going on leave today and I was disappointed. The four Jersey boys have gone now and all the others are gone on leave. We was all going and the sergeant came in the room and told the three of us that we was not for the draft. I'm not sorry in one way for they are going to India and I don't want to go in India. It's too far from home but I was disappointed this morning when I was told I was not going. Dear Lill, you say that in your letter, but I answered all your questions from the letter I had. How are they all at home? I'm a bit downhearted today and how was your engagement and wedding. Best love to my little Mavis and ma and pa, from Edward.'

What became of Edward? Did he survive? With no address (the card was clearly posted in an envelope), we will never know.

Books And Learning: A New Beginning

A building of distinction at the western end of Gosport High Street, the former Public Library and Technical Institute is now Gosport's Local Studies Centre, just across from the town's Discovery Centre – or library, as most people would call it.

Refurbished in its original art nouveau style, it now offers a dedicated centre for local research covering Gosport including Lee-on-the-Solent, plus general Hampshire and the Isle of Wight – a highly appropriate use for a building which was relaunched in the 1970s as Gosport Museum.

School and library were combined in this distinctive High Street building, opened in 1901.

Today the former Public Library and Technical Institute is Gosport's Local Studies Centre.

Before that, it had also been home to Gosport Secondary School, Gosport County School and finally Gosport County Grammar School before the Grammar moved to Bay House at Stokes Bay.

The building, which cost £8,000, was declared open by the Earl of Northbrook in September 1901 – an important day in the history of the changing face of Gosport. The ramparts had been levelled to allow construction, all part of the transformation of this particular quarter.

Demand for the building had been growing for some time. Nine years before, Gosport's inability to train for its own industries had been noted in a pamphlet which argued for the building of a technical school. 'Gosport has been for a hundred years a yacht building port', the document argued. 'There are as well going on sail-making and naval engineering, and the aim is to develop the School in the direction of meeting the needs of these and other smaller industries.'

Right from the start, books and learning were intimately linked in the building, school and library going naturally together and clearly flourishing. By 1911 it was noted: 'The Secondary School is already well-known as a very successful municipal education centre. Its general object is to provide a sound secondary education, on modern lines, for boys and girls above the age of 10 years such as would fit them for an industrial, commercial or professional career.'

It was capable of taking 200 students, though apparently averaged 140. Alongside it, the library boasted around 10,000 volumes. It was staffed by one librarian and two assistants, and the year ending 31 March 1920 saw 49,653 borrowings.

The building's chief feature is perhaps the frieze over the main entrance. Designed by Schenck and executed in cement relief, it depicts the landing in 1158 of Henry of Blois.

Imagine The Days...

In some ways, Gosport distinguishes itself these days by the things it has not got. There cannot be many towns of Gosport's size without a working railway station; without a cinema; or without a theatre. Presumably there are even fewer towns without any of the above – and yet Gosport did, of course, have all three.

The theatre, the attractive red brick building with the pointed roof on the right in these two images, stood in the High Street. It was opened in 1796 by Henry Thornton, a prompter at the theatre in the High Street in Portsmouth who went on to become one of the foremost actor-managers of his day. Thornton operated a theatre circuit which included Andover, Reading, Newbury, Chichester, Croydon, Gosport and elsewhere. Thornton also built the original Theatre Royal in Windsor for George III.

It is believed that Gosport's theatre seated 800 people. Just after the turn of the 19th century, when the venue was perhaps at its peak, a theatre critic wrote: 'The theatre is not excelled by any provincial building. The selection of pieces and the excellence of the performers is exceeded by none.' It is a description which leaves you longing for a glimpse of how the theatre must have looked in its heyday with the crowds coming and going in their finery.

'The selection of pieces and the excellence of the performers is exceeded by none' – so said a critic of the historic theatre in Gosport's High Street.

Estate agents rather than theatrical agents now operate from the former theatre in the High Street.

The theatre closed in 1826 and became a chapel. Later the premises, rather more prosaically, became Timothy Whites and are now home to Ladbrokes betting shop and Blakes estate agents.

Gosport's last professional theatre was also situated on the south side of the High Street but further towards the ferry. It opened in 1924 and produced a new play each week. The building was originally a chapel, then it became a cinema just before World War One and later became Rumbelows.

One of Henry Thornton's most significant other theatres was opened in 1800 in Market Street, Guildford. It was a standard circuit theatre with pit and gallery. It was last used as a theatre in 1861, after which it became a warehouse and was demolished in 1889.

Where It All Happened

Think of the dull uniformity of so much modern architecture, and you just cannot help lamenting Gosport's Thorngate Memorial Hall – a strange piece of Gothic extravagance which brought something slightly exotic to the western end of Gosport High Street.

A building of red brick with stone dressings in the Flemish Gothic style, with stepped gables and flanked in front by two crenellated and domed turrets, it housed Gosport's Town Hall, Council

The Thorngate Memorial Hall and the Drill Hall were High Street landmarks until World War Two.

Gosport Town Hall on the left and the Discovery Centre on the right are rather mundane compared to the buildings which preceded them.

Building and the Memorial Hall. They were distinguished, says the 1911 *Pocket Guide*, putting it rather mildly, by their 'somewhat uncommon design'.

Inside were the office of the Urban District Council, the offices of the Overseers and Board of Guardians and a hall capable of seating nearly 700 people – a venue put to good use when the Gosport versus Alverstoke debate raged, first in the late 19th century and then again during the early 20th century.

Gosport had been governed by the Alverstoke Local Board. When local government reorganisation loomed, Gosportians and the Alverstocracy went to war over its title – and it was in the Thorngate Hall that the ensuing public inquiry was held.

The building took its own name from William Thorngate, a Gosport merchant and philanthropist under whose will the buildings were constructed in 1885. Previously the Alverstoke Local Board offices had been in Stoke Road.

Sadly it was destroyed by enemy action early in the war and remained a pile of rubble for some time even after the advent of peace. The present Town Hall opened in the 1960s and is home to Gosport Borough Council. The name Thorngate lives on in Gosport through the new Thorngate Halls, which were built in Bury Road in the late 1950s for community use – due acknowledgement of a man of great generosity.

Gosport Pays A Heavy Price

Home to Gosport's Conservative Association, the Union building pictured here has, rather like the Local Studies Centre opposite it, watched unchanged as Gosport has changed around it.

The foundation stone was laid on 27 May 1914 by paymaster-in-chief Sir John S. Moore, chairman of the Gosport and Alverstoke Conservative and Unionist Association. Like the Local Studies Centre, it survived World War Two, although plenty of other buildings around it did not. Gosport's historic Congregational Church nearby was destroyed. So too was the Thorngate Memorial Hall just to the

The Union building has remained unchanged for nearly a century in a part of Gosport which has changed dramatically.

left of the Union building – a fate which was repeated time and time again across the borough.

The statistics are grim. 11,000 houses were damaged in Gosport during World War Two, and nearly 500 were destroyed. More than half the town's houses were damaged in some way.

The death toll was similarly ghastly. 111 civilians were killed and 289 wounded. In 61 raids, more than 10,000 incendiaries were dropped on the town. The heaviest raids were 12 and 16 August 1940 and 10 January, 10 March and 14 June 1941. The density of the borough's housing tragically maximised the damage.

There are many terraced roads in Gosport today where you can still see the newer houses replacing those which were reduced to rubble. Queens Road and Avenue Road, off Stoke Road, are examples.

The war left Gosport in a sorry state – one which called for far-sighted local leadership. Fortunately, the borough was in good hands. As early as March 1944, Gosport Corporation was committed to building 1,000 houses on a site in Fareham Road in the first two years of peace. A previous scheme had planned 600 homes, but the forward-thinking Councillor A.R. Nobes urged the local authorities to extend the scheme significantly, urging that Gosport should be ready the moment the Ministry gave the go-ahead.

To the right of the Union building, out of the picture, was Gosport's principal cinema, the Ritz, and it too was severely damaged during the early years of World War Two. Fortunately, it rose again

This building at the western end of the High Street is home to Gosport's Conservative Association.

from the rubble to become a key part of the childhood of post-war youngsters in Gosport. My friends and I would be there almost every Saturday in the late 1970s. *Star Wars* in 1977 was a big event at the Ritz; we all shivered at *The Shining* a couple of years later; and every week we would chant out the words to the unchanging advertisement: 'Sunny Spain? Or maybe Rome? We'll take you there. Davis World Travel of Gosport and Fareham.'

The cinema closed in October 1982, and for years it was fronted by corrugated iron. The joke was that you needed a tin-opener to go to the cinema in Gosport. All too briefly the cinema reopened, only to be demolished in 2001. The site is now occupied by shops and offices.

5. Walpole Park, the Barracks and the Railway

An Open Space In The Heart Of Gosport

Aerial photographs graphically illustrate the way Walpole Park cuts a green swathe across Gosport, offering a breathing space between the once-walled High Street area to the east and Stoke Road to the west.

Linking the two is Walpole Road, and at this point Walpole Park is fairly formal in appearance, offering flower beds and shrub borders. At the end of Walpole Road, on the left as you head into the High Street, is Morrisons supermarket, just where the pedestrianised area begins.

In the past you would have driven in between the library/museum on the left and the Ritz and the Thorngate Hall on your right as you approached the ferry. Now traffic is diverted to the right to join the South Relief Road.

To the left in the modern picture overleaf, just before Morrisons, is where Gosport's driving test centre used to stand until it was knocked down in the late 1980s as part of the area's redevelopment.

As for the Park, it remains an important part of Gosport's fabric, the start and end point for carnival processions and the scene of various youth events.

The section of Walpole Park defined by Walpole Road to the north and the South Relief Road to the south has also served as home to the town's music festival, attracting many top names over the

The leafy elegance of Walpole Park separates Gosport High Street and Stoke Road.

Walpole Park as it is today. Holy Trinity Chuch bell tower can be seen on the right.

years. Music continues here, but these days there is also the Stokes Bay Music Festival a couple of miles away.

Walpole Park has also played host to numerous fun fairs and circuses down the years. I remember a school trip to a circus there in the 1970s when lions were the key attraction – a sign of less enlightened times. The lions had the last laugh, however. One of their number projected a jet of urine into the audience, drenching at least two of my classmates who consequently missed the second half. They were not popular in polite company for quite some time.

Leisure In The Rector's Name

Until the late 1970s when the South Relief Road was cut through it, Walpole Park stretched unbroken down to Alver Creek.

Just to the east of the main part of the Park, adjoining South Street, was Gosport's open-air swimming pool which was opened in 1924: a hard, unforgiving concrete structure which was hardly conducive to fun when we used to trek down there for school swimming galas 30 years and more ago. It is difficult to imagine that too many schoolchildren were greatly grieved when it closed. A car park now occupies the site.

'Much more was expected from this lido than was ever obtained', notes Gosport historian Leonard White. True enough. All we ever got was grazed knees and uncontrollable shivers.

However, other happier water activities are still part of Walpole Park. The old cockle-pond was redesigned for use as a model yacht pond and became a national centre for model yacht racing events. The use has dwindled in more recent years, but Walpole Park is still home to Gosport Model Yacht & Boat Club.

Walpole Park is one of the wealth of parks Gosport has to offer.

A key part of any Gosport childhood in the 1970s was renting rowing boats on the lake and making sure you fell in at some point before your number was called. These days, the swans seem to dominate, backed up by innumerable pigeons. Nearby, part of the provision for youngsters in the area, is a play area with skateboard facilities.

Walpole Park was named after Thomas Walpole. Born on 30 September 1805, he was appointed rector of St Mary's Church, Alverstoke, in 1846 and remained so until his death on 7 February 1881.

Walpole was buried, along with his family, at St Mark's Church which was built in 1844 as part of Robert Cruickshank's development of Angleseyville. One of his sons became librarian of the House of Commons. The church was deemed unsafe in 1911 and pulled down.

Walpole Park takes its name from Thomas Walpole, rector of St Mary's Church, Alverstoke.

Completed in 1859, St George's Barracks were an important part of Gosport's military commitments.

Home To The Armed Forces

Situated to the north of Walpole Park is a reminder of Gosport's military importance – the former St George's Barracks.

It is worth pausing for a moment to consider the extent to which Gosport has been shaped – and for more than two centuries dominated – by the armed forces.

Historians talk of the town being effectively an occupied town during the war, occupied by the navy. But it goes further than that.

In the 1960s in Gosport you could have counted something like 20 establishments, both navy and army, occupying perhaps a third of the peninsula's land area. In the past few decades, however, considerable amounts of that land have been freed up, mostly for housing, as the armed forces have withdrawn.

At the peak of their involvement, Gosport was home to the Royal Naval Training Establishment at St Vincent, the Royal Clarence Victualling Yard, the Royal Naval Mining School at Bedenham, the Royal Naval Hospital at Haslar, the Royal Naval Aircraft Repair Yard at Fleetlands, HMS Sultan Royal Naval School of Engineering, the Royal Naval Ordnance Depot at Priddy's Hard, HMS Dolphin submarine base and the Royal Naval Air Station at Lee-on-the-Solent.

Also in the borough was the army at St George's Barracks, originally known as Gosport Barracks or New Barracks. A century ago, a Gosport guide book stated: 'Some idea of Gosport's importance in the military world will be obtained by a visit to the Barracks which stretches from the end of High Street to beyond the Clarence Victualling Yard gates, the total frontage being nearly 600 yards.'

St George's Barracks are barracks no more.

Begun at the time of the Crimean War, construction of the barracks was completed in 1859, providing accommodation for 1,000 men plus quarters for officers and NCOs – a product of the anxious 1800s when it was felt that Gosport needed further fortification. Situated just outside the old ramparts, the barracks acted as a reserve to defend the newly-created line of forts at Browndown, Gomer, Rowner, Grange, Brockhurst and Elson.

During World War Two, the barracks were taken over by the Admiralty, but they returned to army use in 1947 when they became home to the 3rd Royal Tank Regiment and gained the name St George's Barracks. Their last army occupants were 20 Maritime Regiment, Royal Corps of Transport who arrived in 1971 and remained there until 1991, when the buildings became surplus to requirements.

The former barracks have now been sold for development which seems sad to me as I still fondly remember being taken there in the 1970s for the army's celebrated curry lunches when Colonel Barratt was in charge. For the two years my father was Mayor of Gosport (1974–76), the curry lunches were one of the few civic events my brother and I were happy to find ourselves dragged along to.

Manning The Fortifications

Pre-dating St George's Barracks but again part of Gosport's 19th-century military expansion are Forton Barracks (1807–1923), the single biggest trigger for the transformation of the former hamlet of Forton.

Forton Barracks were an important part of Gosport's 19th-century military expansion.

*Today the barracks are
home to St Vincent College.*

The farmers and millers of old Forton provided the fresh produce for the victualling yards which developed on the eastern town side of the village during the 18th and 19th centuries. But with the building of the barracks in the early 1800s, that rural character started to erode.

Originally the barracks were to have been a new prison hospital, but with Haslar Hospital a mile or so away more than adequately fulfilling its purpose, the need was never really there. The designs were changed, and the present barracks began to take shape, described in contemporary accounts as having 'four very lofty pavilions, connected by arcades of great extent with a parade ground of some area.'

The barracks were soon put to good use, the men based there manning the town's fortifications and also running the prison hulks in Forton Creek. With the new men came greater demands on Forton, which grew to include homes for married soldiers, plus a range of shops and – inevitably – pubs.

An important change at the barracks came in 1848 when the Royal Marine Light Infantry – known as the Red Marines – moved in, leaving behind Clarence Barracks, their home since 1765. The barracks expanded during the second half of the 19th century, with parts of the foreshore reclaimed, an open-air swimming pool built and a theatre added. At one point the parade ground was probably the largest in the country.

The marines, who had by then acquired a lasting tribute in the shape of Gosport's War Memorial Hospital, departed in 1923 when they were amalgamated with the Royal Marine Artillery and moved to their new home at Eastney.

The barracks then became HMS St Vincent Boys' Training Establishment from 1927–65. The Navy moved out in 1968 and in the mid-1970s the barracks became St Vincent School. They are now Gosport and Fareham's sixth-form college, St Vincent College.

When The Railway Came

The roof and the lines have long since gone, but despite the years of unforgivable neglect, there is no denying the fact that Gosport railway station has maintained a certain grandeur – against all the odds

What will become of the site remains to be seen, but it is surely a tragedy that nothing more has been made of it since the station closed more than half a century ago, bringing to an end an important passage in Gosport's history.

It was recognition of the town's growing significance in 1841 when the London and South Western Railway Company bought property in Spring Garden Lane belonging to Mr Isaac Legg in order to build a station, which was officially opened on 7 February 1842, ushering in a century of passenger service by rail.

With intermediate stations at Botley and Fareham, this was a branch of the Southampton line, launching six years before the first station opened in Portsmouth.

The line stopped at Spring Garden Lane, prevented by Gosport's fortifications from getting closer to the harbour. But the railway was not restricted in other respects, and the town's stations multiplied as the century advanced.

The railway reached Gosport in 1841. The town's new station was the envy of many.

Today, Gosport station is in a sorry condition as it awaits its future.

The Stokes Bay line opened in 1863, branching off the main line in Stoke Road to run down to the pier at Stokes Bay and passing over the railway bridge at Haslar Creek, where it enjoyed much-vaunted views across the water to Alverstoke village.

A station was opened in Stoke Road, another was added in Brockhurst two years later, and in the 1890s the network was extended to Lee-on-the-Solent with intermediate stations at Privett and Browndown. The Lee branch included a station at Elmore.

There was also a station in Clarence Yard enabling Queen Victoria to board the Royal Yacht for her journeys to Osborne House.

The Rise And Fall Of The Railways

At the bottom of Spring Garden Lane is the ruin of Gosport's railway station. In the recent photograph (see previous page) it is a sad shell, inaccessible and in poor condition; in the earlier photograph it would have been bustling with life.

In Gosport's mid-Victorian railway heyday, trains travelling at 20mph were advertised. The cost of a single fare to London ranged from 8/6 in an open wagon to 22/- on the fast train.

The railway timetable for May 1894, produced to incorporate the new Lee-on-the-Solent railway, makes interesting reading. If you left Gosport at 9.39am, you could be in London Waterloo at 12.18pm. If you factor in the ferry crossing to Portsmouth you would have to make today simply to catch the train in the first place, the time compares reasonably favourably with current rail travel.

Transport was horse-drawn in this enchanting image of Spring Garden Lane.

At the beginning of Walpole Park, Spring Garden Lane leads to Gosport's disused railway station.

Designed by William Tite (1798–1873), Gosport's railway station was hailed as one of the most impressive structures of its kind outside London, built in the Italianate classic tradition and finished with Tuscan columns with Corinthian capitals.

Tite's greatest achievement was perhaps the rebuilding of the Royal Exchange in London which opened in 1844, but he was also closely associated with railway stations – and many survive.

Tite was the man behind the Southampton Terminus, Windsor Riverside, Carnforth station and Carlisle Citadel station, plus the majority of the stations on the Caledonian and Scottish Central railways, including Edinburgh and Perth.

And with his design for Gosport, he did the town proud. It looked fit for royalty and clearly was, with the Royal Family first using it in 1843. Soon afterwards, the Queen bought the Osborne estate on the Isle of Wight, cementing Gosport's importance to Albert and Victoria.

But even at its peak, the seeds had been sown for Gosport's eventual railway decline. Portsmouth's railway station opened in 1847, and this soon began to take a toll on Gosport's railway fortunes. By the dawn of the new century, the downturn had set in, soon to be accelerated by the popularity of the new tramway system.

The Stokes Bay branch was the first to go, closed to public traffic in 1915, with the Lee branch following suit at the end of 1930. Gosport station was used by the military during the war, but it suffered air-raid damage and never really recovered. It too was closed to passengers in 1953. The final nail in the coffin for Gosport's railway network came in 1969 when the whole railway south of the Admiralty siding at Bedenham was abandoned.

6. From Stoke Road to Bury Road

Sad Times For The Town's Pubs

Heading west from the High Street and passing through Walpole Park, you enter the top end of Stoke Road which has been a shopping area since Victorian times. It escaped the pedestrianisation which was inflicted on the High Street in the late 20th century, but sadly free flow of traffic does not seem to have meant free flow of business. Stoke Road is home to more empty shops than you would care to see. Some of the vacant premises have stood vacant for years. It is fair to say that Stoke Road these days looks fairly run-down.

One of the saddest losses in recent times is The Royal Arms public house, seen on the right of this lovely early 20th-century image of Stoke Road, which must date from before 1908 when the pub's characteristic canopy was added.

It is an image rich in detail, with the women grouped around the pram to the right, the young men, hats on heads, loitering by the roadside, the tram and its tracks dominating the street scene and the horse-drawn carriage to the left.

Believed to have been the last public house in Gosport to brew its own beer, The Royal Arms is now boarded up – a sad sign of the times. Recently two pubs at the end of Ann's Hill Road and three in Brockhurst Road have also closed.

Stoke Road bustles busily in this turn-of-the-century image. The Royal Arms public house is on the right.

Like so many of Gosport's pubs, The Royal Arms fell on hard times and closed in recent years. Its distinctive canopy, absent in the earlier photograph, is starting to look its age.

In the summer of 2009, the full extent of the decline in our pubs was made worryingly clear when it emerged that pubs are closing in record numbers – a result of the combined impact of the recession, rises in beer duty and the smoking ban. Seven pubs are closing every day, according to the British Beer & Pub Association. Fifty-two pubs closed on average every week in the first six months of 2009, a third up on the already disturbing figures announced for the last half of 2008.

The Heyday Of The Tram

How many trees are there in Stoke Road now? Not many. The road has lost the almost country aspect it enjoys in the early image overleaf of the days when trams, not cars, ruled the roads.

Electric trams took over from horse trams in Gosport in 1906 and were in turn replaced by buses at the end of 1929 with the closure of the Gosport and Fareham Tramways. In Portsmouth, trams continued running until 1936, when Portsmouth Corporation Tramways followed suit and closed their final route.

The first trams in the area had been operated by Portsmouth Street Tramways, opening in May 1865; just over 40 years later, a service began in Gosport. The rolling stock consisted of 22 four-wheel, double-deck, open-top cars, and the fare was 3d to Brockhurst, 6d to Fareham.

The tramways were the property of the Gosport and Fareham Tramways Company. After it closed, some of the tramcars were redeployed locally; others went to the Great Grimsby system.

The demise of the tram in Gosport was part of a national trend. London scrapped its tram network in 1952, and within 10 years just about every other major British city had said goodbye to the tram.

Recent years have seen much talk about a possible tram revival, but it has yet to happen, and in 2003 Alistair Darling, the then Transport Secretary, refused to approve a tram line linking

The tram rules the roads in this postcard of Stoke Road, dating from around 1910.

Saturday evening in Stoke Road today.

Portsmouth and Gosport via a tunnel under the harbour after the estimated costs rose £100 million in just 18 months to £270 million.

Cities on the Continent love their trams, but British transport planners are not convinced. As *The Times* wryly observed 'To them, the streetcar is not named desire'.

Favourite Childhood Places

To the children of the 1960s there were only two places worth bothering with in Stoke Road. One was Nobes, a shop which offered a combination dreamt up in heaven – sports gear downstairs and toys upstairs. The other was Bulls, seen on the left-hand side in the earlier image (opposite), a hardware store which was a genuine emporium. Run in the 1970s by Roger Duffett, who happened to live next door to us in Beech Grove, the shop was an absolute treasure trove, capable of pleasing everyone.

The kitchenware and garden sections effectively catered for your parents, leaving you to enjoy a toy section which, though smaller, rivalled Nobes in many respects and certainly exceeded it when it came to kitting out your Action Man.

Housed at the start of Portland Buildings, it was a worthy use of a very elegant building – part of an attractive stretch on the northern side of Stoke Road.

For years, Stoke Road was the home of the Olympia, a little further up on the corner of Queens Road. It opened as a skating rink in the early 1920s and became a music hall and eventually a cinema. Chichester's first cinema was also an Olympia, also combined with a skating rink. Its building still stands, looking sadly dilapidated, but in Gosport, like the Ritz, the Olympia has long since gone.

Other shops nearby in the 1930s included Claude S. March, household linen draper; H.H. Thatcher & Co, wine and spirit merchants; and Pimm & Willy Ltd, motor garage. But one of the

Portland Buildings are on the left in this image of Stoke Road. On the right are a number of sailors, so frequently to be seen in past postcards of Gosport.

A present-day view of Stoke Road. Portland Buildings are unchanged, but there are some changes to the shops on the right.

most colourful must surely have been Gurden & Co, the Gosport florists and fruiterers who promised wreaths, crosses, wedding bouquets and sprays, all the latest designs 'at a moment's notice' – 'everything for a successful garden supplied; experienced gardeners sent out daily'. Their premises at 6 Portland Buildings are now occupied by the music shop Just Music.

It Used To Be So Rural...

Another Stoke Road tram scene, and another image of a Stoke Road considerably leafier than it is today. Where there were trees on the right in this 1907 postcard, there is now a row of shops including Blockbusters film rental outlet and Waitrose (see overleaf). On the left, however, The Vine still stands. Dating from 1840, the pub once had its own pleasure grounds and tea rooms, and it is seen here in an image which underlines Stoke Road's rural roots.

Much of the northern side of Stoke Road used to comprise fields and orchards, and in the 1700s the road was a simple cart track, a link between ancient Alverstoke and the newer town of Gosport which was about to embark on an era of rapid growth.

The carts with their hay stacked high have long since gone, but the area's countryside past lives on in some of the street names in the area such as Stoke Gardens, Oak Street and Holly Street.

Stoke Road presents a leafy aspect on this postcard, which was sent in 1907.

Parts of the Stoke Road area have been enhanced with finance from Hampshire County Council from the Urban Regeneration Fund. Conservation Area status is a protection elsewhere. And in recent years £510,000 has been spent on improvements to the shopping area by Hampshire County Council and Gosport Borough Council. But the truth is that this western end of Stoke Road, like the eastern end, still does not seem particularly vibrant.

Barely a tree in sight in this present-day image of Stoke Road.

The consolation is that at least Stoke Road retains a decent number of individual shops, unlike the High Street which is home to a mix of banks, chain stores, charity shops and discount outlets. Traditional family firms still survive in Stoke Road in a way they do not in the High Street, and it consequently bills itself as Gosport's specialist shopping area.

All Change At Gosport Road Station

There are plenty of differences to explore between these two images of The White Hart pub at the western end of Stoke Road (see page 99).

The pub has been rebuilt in a slightly different position, and of Bury Arch on the right (demolished in 1938) no sign remains, nothing to indicate that this was once raised ground over which trams passed.

Behind the pub was Gosport Road station. Initially it was Stoke Road station, but the Gosport designation was generally accepted for the railway link to Stokes Bay. The line, which can now be followed on foot or by bike, was opened in 1863 and closed to passenger traffic in 1915.

Behind the pub, where there used to be a railway footbridge, now runs the South Relief Road, which opened in 1979 and remains one of the most significant Gosport road changes in recent years, linking up with South Street not long before the new Haslar Bridge made the creek passable by car for the first time in generations.

Other well-known railway footbridges were on the Daisy Lane corner, the Lees Lane corner and at the bottom of Albert Street. By the time my father was a child, they had become glorified climbing frames and were eventually demolished.

Nothing in this image of The White Hart remains today.

Back to the earlier postcard of The White Hart, though, and there is another little reminder of the ephemeral nature of all things mortal.

Written to Mr Carr, of Lake Road, Portsmouth, in February 1927, it runs: 'We hope, as we have not seen you, that you have escaped la grippe. Harry did four days in the yard before he had a

The railway bridge has gone and the pub has been rebuilt.

relapse, but he struggled on till they sent him home. Three weeks ago he was dreadfully bad and I had the two girls till when he came back. Mary was very ill. It went to her heart but she is getting on now. Harry has gone away to see what that will do for him. He is in Cambridge now, went off on Monday morning, and we are getting better news of him so I do hope it will do him good.'

Just a decade earlier, almost nowhere on earth had escaped the Spanish flu pandemic. Most of its victims were healthy young adults. Estimates vary wildly, but it seems somewhere between 50 to 100 million people died worldwide.

Going To School

At The White Hart, Stoke Road becomes Bury Road. Follow it away from the town centre, and after a quarter of a mile or so you pass the town end of Green Lane, shown in the following two

photographs. At its other end once stood Alverstoke National School, and it is just possible that the group of children in the early photograph below are walking home from a hard day in the classroom.

Again it is a photograph rich in detail. Green Lane was my route to Leesland School in the early 1970s, and it is a lovely thought that these earlier children, looking far smarter than we ever did, walked it 60 years before.

The small boy in the middle is clearly posing for the camera; so too perhaps is the girl on the left. The others in the group are less self-conscious, lending the image an easy charm which you would struggle to find in Green Lane now. In my schooldays it was fairly universally known by the crudest of nicknames, reflecting defecating dogs and the carelessness of their 1970s owners.

These children may well have been returning from Alverstoke National School in this evocative archive image.

Today, Green Lane remains a popular, leafy cut-through connecting Bury Road with Anglesey Road.

But even now, it still retains something of its rural character, with well-established plants and trees behind the high fences. Earlier postcards show it to be virtually countryside. One image in my father's collection, from the days when the fences were considerably lower, shows a huge haystack on the left-hand side – a long time ago, clearly before the use of postcards became a regular part of life. On the back, the sender wrote the address across both halves of the blank area, plus the words 'Happy Christmas'. On the front, above the image of the haystack, he scrawled 'Greetings from Gosport'. The card is dated 22 December 1906.

Remembering The War Dead

Gosport's tribute to the dead of World War One is the hospital which has stood in Bury Road since the early 1920s. Built by public subscription, it also stands as the official memorial to the Royal Marine Light Infantry who enjoyed a long association with Gosport. From their barracks at St Vincent they contributed generously to the hospital scheme. The sad irony is that they moved out of Gosport in 1923 so soon after the hospital was built.

The foundation stone was laid in July 1921 by Field Marshal Earl Haig, the commander of the British Expeditionary Force from 1915 through to the German surrender in 1918. Haig – created 1st Earl Haig after the war – was commander during the Battle of the Somme and the Third Battle of Ypres. Historians will probably never agree to what extent the final victory was his, but after the armistice he devoted the rest of his life to the welfare of ex-servicemen.

My late grandmother, who lived less than a mile away from the new hospital, was incapable of mentioning his name without adding the word 'butcher', but laying the foundation stone would have been typical of his post-war work – and a coup for Gosport.

The only building of importance erected in town in the years immediately following World War One, the hospital was completed in April 1923 and gained its clock – for which a gable was added

Gosport's War Memorial Hospital honoured the dead of World War One.

– in 1950. In the mid-1990s, the hospital was substantially extended, with a major new wing added to the rear of the main hospital building.

The hospital has recently hosted a re-dedication ceremony to unveil a new war memorial stone. Attending the service were standard bearers from the Royal British Legion and two buglers from the Royal Marines who played The Last Post and Reveille.

The front of the hospital is largely unchanged today, but the hospital has been significantly expanded at the back.

In the early years of the 20th century The Wiltshire Lamb was an important terminus in Gosport's public transport network.

The Silence Of The Wiltshire Lamb

Another Gosport pub to have fallen by the wayside is The Wiltshire Lamb, yet another victim of a pub industry in crisis. It is a sad loss. The Wiltshire Lamb had a proud history, serving and supporting the Bury Cross tram terminus, as depicted in this older postcard.

Today, The Wiltshire Lamb is simply yet another boarded-up pub.

Written to a Miss Bundy, of Winchester, in 1922, it offered a festive message to 'Dear Nelly. What beastly weather for Xmas. I do hope it will be brighter altho' it is jolly being here with them all. How are you keeping? I hope free from that wretched toothache. I suppose you are ready for Christmas now, mind you. Pull the doll's fastenings on his clothes. With every good wish for Christmas and the New Year. I remain yours sincerely M. Fairs.'

As for the image, it's another where the past looks so much more appealing than the present.

At the end of the tram line, The Wiltshire Lamb was conveniently situated to provide weary travellers with refreshments. Car No. 3 of the Gosport and Fareham Tramways Company awaits departure. A woman and a child, presumably her daughter, look on.

The original intention was that the tram route should be extended to Lee-on-the-Solent but this never happened, and Bury Cross was as far as it went. In the event, this was the first line to be abandoned.

To the right is the start of Ann's Hill Road leading to Ann's Hill Cemetery, which has the slightly bizarre distinction that part of an episode of *Taggart* was filmed there in the early 1990s.

Back to Bury Road, and a few hundred yards further along on the left stood the Bury Cross waterworks, a nearby landmark with its famous tower, just past the turning into Jellicoe Avenue. Built in the 1850s, it was demolished in 1970.

7. Lee-on-the-Solent

Creating A New Resort

It sounds rather damning to say that Lee-on-the-Solent is essentially a failed seaside resort which found its niche instead as a residential centre. But arguably it is true, and it is surely a tribute that people want to live there rather than simply visit.

Approached from Gosport in the following two images, Lee offers obvious attractions – a safe, gentle shoreline lined by attractive accommodation.

Although the name Lee goes back to the 13th century, Lee-on-the-Solent is a much more recent invention, all part of a late-Victorian attempt to create a watering-hole to bring in the visitors.

The name was first touted in 1884 when Sir John Robinson, a wealthy Dorset landowner, set out his vision for a new seaside resort on lands mainly in the ancient Manor of Lee Britten, approximately three miles from Gosport. Sir John's son, Mr C.E. Newton Robinson, had been the man to see its potential first while yachting in the area. It pleased him and so he persuaded his father to invest in it. Sir John obediently bought the foreshore.

There was a genuine sense that something new was being created, as a report from *The Evening News* dated 1885 makes clear: 'The development of this young watering-place is progressing so

For many years Lee Tower was a familiar sea-front landmark. It was demolished in 1971.

Lee-on-the-Solent's sea-front is characterised by attractive residential development.

rapidly that whereas a year ago the name was scarcely known, in another year's time it is probable that a town will be built upon the land that is now called Lee-on-the-Solent.'

The *Portsmouth Times* even sent reporters to investigate 'the projected new marine town'. They lauded its 'fortunate locality'.

Work on Lee Pier – the remains of which can be seen, detached from the mainland, in the earlier photograph – began almost immediately, part of the UK's pier-building heyday. But significant residential development did not really get going until the early years of the 20th century. By the 1920s and 1930s, things were really taking off – in 1930s style. And these were the years which shaped Lee's character.

The art deco Marine Parade, facing the sea, dates from the 1930s, and facing it, so did Lee Tower, a familiar landmark which dominates the skyline in the earlier image and still seems strangely absent in the more recent one, nearly 40 years after its demolition.

By now a seaside resort, Lee-on-the-Solent was incorporated into the Borough of Gosport in 1930, eight years after Gosport gained borough status, but even today Lee remains quite distinct from the town itself.

At The End Of The Rainbow

Lee Tower was promised as 'where the rainbow ends'. Sadly, it was never quite that.

Nikolas Pevsner damned it with the faintest of praise in his architectural guide to Hampshire when he called it 'a good piece of second-rate inter-war modernism of the slightly jazzy sort, constructed of concrete when concrete seemed very up-to-date', describing the tower itself as looking 'rather like an elongated cigarette lighter.'

Over the years, it became uneconomic to maintain and was demolished in 1971; although in hindsight many people would argue that it should have been seen as an investment for the

Lee Tower was supposed to be 'where the rainbow ends'. Sadly, it never was.

This is where Lee Tower stood, and there are many who wish it still did.

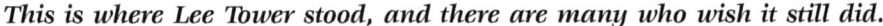

future, especially when you consider the current success of the Spinnaker Tower on Portsmouth waterfront.

Today the site is occupied by the promenade and remembrance gardens – attractive enough, but certainly not the magnet a properly-maintained tower might once again have become.

The tower complex, built in the 1930s in bold art deco style, housed a cinema, a ballroom and other leisure activities, but its principal feature was, of course, the tower, which was distinctive, 120ft tall and enjoyed superb views.

There was a time when all the significant events in the borough were held in the tower buildings, from mayor-making through to the visits of various dignitaries. It was also a popular place for wedding receptions. My parents held theirs there in 1961. They had the top-of-the-range four-course menus at 9/6 per head and hired a Provincial bus to transport the guests to the tower from Fareham's Holy Trinity Church.

An attempt was made in 1964 to revive the tower's flagging fortunes when the cinema was turned into a bowling alley, but it was too little too late and demolition followed seven years later.

Just out of shot to the left in the more recent image is an amusement arcade in a building which was once the booking hall for Lee railway station. Nothing else remains of the station, which closed in 1930 – five years before the tower complex was built.

Taking The Sea Air

Protruding into the sea at the foot of Lee Tower was Lee Pier, a product of a time when a pier was an essential accessory for any self-respecting seaside resort.

Like so many would-be fashionable resorts, Lee-on-the-Solent boasted a pier.

Like Lee Tower, Lee Pier is now just a memory.

The Victorians were the great pier-builders, and Lee Pier was part of that great pier-building heyday. Built in the 1880s, it was 750ft long and for years fared well, offering a regular steamer service to Southsea. It was also a stopping-off point for the paddle steamers which ran between Southampton, Stokes Bay, Cowes and Ryde Piers.

A charming newspaper advertisement from the 1890s recommends Lee-on-the-Solent as 'a pleasant sea trip of about 45 minutes from Southsea Pier.'

Leaving Gosport Hard at 9.30am, the 'safe and excellent sea-boat' *Venus* reached Portsea and Harbour Station at 9.40, arrived at Portsmouth Pier at 9.45, reached Southsea Pier at 9.50 and departed at 10 on its way to Stokes Bay Pier, where it arrived at 10.25 before sailing to Lee-on-the-Solent Pier where it arrived at 10.50. There it waited for 10 minutes before returning to Stokes Bay. It then spent the rest of the day sailing between Southsea, Stokes Bay and Lee before finally returning to Gosport Hard at 7.15pm.

Sadly the pier's fortunes nosedived in 1932 when a fire destroyed the ballroom and restaurant at its far end. The pier then stood semi-derelict for many years, before the war hammered another nail into its coffin. With the outbreak of war the military authorities breached the pier as a precaution against invasion, and it was never rebuilt – though the US army repaired it sufficiently to use it as a launching stage during the D-Day landings.

By then the pier's glory days were well and truly over, and it was eventually demolished in 1958.

As the National Piers Society notes, at the turn of the 20th century, almost 100 piers existed. Sadly, now only half remain and several face an uncertain future. Each was a testament to the achievements of Victorian engineers and entrepreneurs.

The Robinsons, who founded Lee-on-the-Solent, had promoted it as a health resort, and the pier had clearly been key to their plans – a pleasant promenade from which to savour the health-giving sea air.

Nearby, without even having to enter the sea, you could enjoy the sea water. The Lido at Lee, built during the 1930s, was believed to be the only open-air heated seawater bathing pool in England.

Seaside Shopping With Elegance

Comfortably one of the most attractive rows of shops in Lee-on-the-Solent predates the art deco buildings which characterised Lee in the 1930s.

The eastern side of Pier Street, linking Marine Parade and Lee High Street as they run parallel to the sea, is Edwardian and charming. Comprising the odd numbers from 1 to 23, the buildings offer a timber balustrade balcony, high-pitched roof and full dormers – fine architectural details in a commercial stretch which has fared remarkably well down the decades.

One might baulk a little at the timber in-filling in the first premises on the left, now a physiotherapy clinic, but otherwise Pier Street's odd numbers have survived more or less intact.

This section of Pier Street was part of the first flush of construction which created Lee Pier (1885–88), part of the package aimed at cementing the new resort's appeal.

Pier Street was always one of Lee's more attractive shopping areas. It is seen here on a postcard sent in 1910.

PIER STREET. LEA-ON-SOLENT

It is remarkable how little Pier Street has changed.

By the 1930s, W. Pink & Son, high-class grocers to the sailing fraternity, occupied the unit now home to the physiotherapy clinic; nearby was Bettina Café, run by proprietor Harry Williams offering 'refreshments &c'. Confectioner Mrs Margaret Houghton also operated from the Edwardian terrace. Nearby were the Vidian Tea Rooms and Tea Gardens, advertised as 'close to the pier' and 'convenient for all weathers, everything home-made.'

The earlier image was sent as a postcard to the delightfully named Miss May Peppercorn, of Girton College, Cambridge on 13 February 1910 as something of a pot-boiler, with the promise of more.

'Dear May, received your letter. I am sorry I have not wrote to you before but I have been so busy. I will send you a letter one day next week. Hope you are well. So good bye, with love from Flo.'

A Resort In Decline

Things have changed rather more radically in the following views of Pier Street.

Pier Street was just yards from Lee Pier and the railway station, but these are behind the photographer in this early image. Here the photographer has turned his back to the sea for an altogether different perspective – one which underlines the extent to which Lee-on-the-Solent was still very much a work in progress when the terraced east side of Pier Street was constructed.

To judge from the earlier photograph, there simply was not a west side. The art deco movement of the 1930s had not arrived. And nor, to any great extent, had the car. Parked cars are everywhere these days, but in the earlier image there is just the one, sitting innocuously beside the greenery.

PIER ST. LEE-ON-SOLENT.

Pier Street is seen from the sea end in this attractive archive image.

The changes are all on the left-hand side in the present-day image.

It all suggests the quieter days from which Lee emerged, taking its name from the river Lee which ran from Peel Common into the Solent. The river lent its name to three hamlets it passed through. Two of them, Lower Lee and Middle Lee, became Lee-on-the-Solent. The third, Upper Lee, became Peel Common.

During its late Victorian expansion and into the 20th century, Lee gained a number of key hotels, but the advent of package holidays abroad in the 1950s and 1960s was one of a number of factors which dented Lee-on-the-Solent's popularity, along with that of so many other south-coast resorts.

These days the hotels have gone, most notably the Belle Vue Hotel after local objections put paid to its planned expansion. In recent years, new developments in Lee have been wholly residential and mainly directed towards the retirement market.

The view among many is that the shops in the High Street have deteriorated, partly because of a lack of visitors, partly because of the increase in out-of-town shopping. Lee's shops no longer have the vibrancy or the individuality they once had – perhaps a reflection of the fact that many younger people feel they have been pushed out of the village by the way it has developed.

Lee-on-the-Solent. 5082.

F. Bulson's emporium on the corner of Manor Way was the Woolworth's of its day.

Controversy Rages

Many people in Lee reacted with a shrug of the shoulders to the locality's character-changing growth spurt; indeed many incomers to Lee are part of that expansion.

But not everyone has been welcomed so quietly into the Lee fold. In 2003, Lee-on-the-Solent found itself at the centre of national controversy when the government announced plans to house asylum-seekers in Lee's former HMS Daedalus base, which was set up as a seaplane base in 1917 and closed as a naval establishment in 1996.

The Daedalus Action Group was formed in February 2003 and fought a vigorous campaign against the proposed open asylum-seekers processing centre – an issue which sharply divided opinion and saw emotions rise.

A view on the website of Gosport's Conservative Association spoke for many: 'Lee-on-the-Solent is an example of a British community, a little old-world perhaps. The values and the very atmosphere speak of England and the way of life that is sadly under threat from the imposition of other cultures that are not understood and who do not understand us.'

Others saw things differently. Appalled at what they considered anti-asylum rhetoric, a group of Lee-on-the-Solent residents set up an opposing group called Neighbour Lee.

In the end, the Daedalus Action Group won the day. On 3 February 2004 the Home Office announced the decision not to proceed with the proposed processing centre. The Action Group continued to monitor the site for the next four years and then wound itself up on 28 September 2008.

The large overhanging tree may have gone, but Manor Way remains pleasantly leafy in this present-day image.

The earlier image shown on the previous page harks back to a time before such controversies, and it shows F. Bulson's emporium on the corner of Manor Way. An equivalent to Woolworth's, it is a reminder of what Lee was like before significant residential development took away its village feel.

8. Gosport's Churches

Victorian Gothic At Its Best

Dominating the Alverstoke skyline and visible from the sea is St Mary's Church, prominently positioned within the Alverstoke Village Conservation Area.

The first known reference to the church's existence is dated 1122. It is just possible that a Saxon church stood on the site of the Norman church which was built in 1625. The present building, however, is much more recent.

Regarded as a fine example of Victorian Gothic, the church is listed by the Ministry of the Environment as a building of special architectural or historic interest. As the *Victoria County History* noted in 1908: 'The Church of Our Lady, Alverstoke, has been gradually rebuilt, and it is now entirely modern.' The roof was raised in the early 1800s and a gallery built at the west end. The chancel dates from 1865 and the nave from 1885, part of the church's staged rebuilding.

The tower, seen here, was added in 1905 as a memorial to the restoration of peace after the South African War. The tower houses a clock with dials on the north and south sides plus eight bells, five of which were added in 1919 in memory of the men of the parish who died in World War One.

A building of stone in the Early English style, comprising a chancel, a nave of five bays, aisles and a western tower 80ft in height, it stands where Gosport began – at the heart of the ancient village which established the borough we know today.

St Mary's Church stands proud on the Alverstoke skyline.

ALVERSTOKE CHURCH, GOSPORT.

The setting seems rather more urban now, but St Mary's Church remains reassuringly and solidly unchanged.

The church, situated near the head of the creek which stretches a mile westwards from Portsmouth Harbour, once served a large, mainly agricultural parish stretching as far as the town at the harbour end of Gosport. Holy Trinity, at the opposite end of the creek, became a separate parish in 1860.

A Rich Interior

Inside as well as outside, St Mary's Church is a fascinating building, and the interior – seen in these two images around 80 years apart – offers a wealth of treasures to explore.

Worthy of inspection is the fascinating collection of kneelers which commemorate much of Gosport's history, recalling institutions, establishments and organisations long since gone.

Most interesting of all perhaps is simply to read the memorials the church contains, very much a testimony to Gosport's military and Empire past.

With the inscription cramped and the words strangely split and abbreviated, one of the very earliest memorials reads: 'Neare this piller lye the body of Capt Edwd Douer commander of his Magistes ship the Expedition whoe departed this life November 17 1696 aged 45.'

Nearby is the memorial to Joseph Larcom, a captain of the Royal Navy and for several years naval commissioner of the island of Malta, who died on 17 February 1818, aged 54, at Gibraltar 'while on his passage to England and was there buried.'

The memorials inside St Mary's Church offer a wealth of fascinating inscriptions.

A century later, Vice-Admiral Frank Hannam Henderson died, on 26 June 1918, aged 68, 'while nobly serving his country in command of convoys.'

Also commemorated is Aiskew Paffard Hollis, Vice-Admiral of the White (1764–1844), 'whose naval career included 70 years of his life, 52 of which were devoted to the active duties of his profession.'

Unsurprisingly, the interior of St Mary's Church seems to have altered little.

Among the most moving is the memorial tablet to Edward Archdale McCurdy, lieutenant-colonel in the Madras Army who died in the East Indies on 28 December 1843, aged 43: 'In him were united all the noble qualities that make the Soldier conspicuous, all the amiable and social virtues that make the Man beloved. Those who were so fortunate to possess his friendship deeply deplore his loss.'

On the north wall is a list of the names of all the Rectors of Alverstoke from 1290 until the present day.

Distinguished Men Remembered

Alverstoke's close connections with the sea are in evidence once again in the graveyard which borders St Mary's Church to the west and north.

Many of the graves have been weathered beyond the point of easy reading, but others retain their fine carvings and fulsome inscriptions, and these readily reward a little bit of on-all-fours research.

Just near the lych gate is the grave of Captain John Bligh 'of His Majesty's Navy who died the 19th of January 1795, aged 59.' Sir Richard Rodney Bligh, KGCB Admiral of the Red, is also interred there, as is Captain G.M. Bligh. The Bligh family is reputed to have been distantly related to the more celebrated Captain Bligh of the *Bounty*.

Also buried in the churchyard is David Bogue, one of the founders of what became the London Missionary Society and a man influential in Gosport's spiritual life in the late 1700s. On his tombstone in St Mary's Church, Alverstoke, are the words: 'Here rests one who in life never rested.' Born in Scotland, he lived from 18 February 1750 to 25 October 1825 and is remembered in Gosport as 'a distinguished citizen of this town.'

St Mary's churchyard is the final resting place for a number of distinguished Gosport citizens.

The railings around the churchyard have recently been restored, as this current image shows.

Numbering more than 500, the graves in St Mary's churchyard date back to the mid-1600s. The graveyard was extended three times in the mid to late 1700s and even acquired a supplementary graveyard off Green Road just after the turn of the 19th century. This lasted until the mid-1850s, when it was superseded by Ann's Hill Cemetery a couple of miles away.

The more recent image shows the results of the restoration of the church's setting, an initiative which relied on historic photographs and local reminiscences. The scheme brought together the Church of St Mary, Alverstoke, the Diocese of Portsmouth, Gosport Borough Council and Alec Peever (stone lettering). It was completed in 2005 and involved refurbishing the lych gate and replacing the railings, which had been removed during World War Two. Their return has not met with universal approval, however, and certainly they look rather stark in the present-day photograph.

Surviving The War

One of the most significant and interesting buildings at the town end of Gosport is Holy Trinity Church, with its prominent landmark campanile and fine interior.

The church, a brick building consisting of a chancel, a nave with aisles of eight bays, a west porch and a detached north-west tower, grew out of the development of the harbour end of Gosport. It relieved the pressure on St Mary's Church in Alverstoke, but more importantly provided a much closer place of worship for people living in the town.

The man behind it was Captain Henry Player, who acquired the site which was then just wild gorse and common land known as Gosport Common. Pillars were provided by the Bishop of Winchester who sent 14 oak trees from his estates at Farnham, and the foundation was laid in 1694. It was consecrated in September 1696 as the Church of the Holy and Undivided Trinity by the Bishop of Winchester.

The church was fire-damaged during World War Two, and much of the area nearby was destroyed. Indeed, it was near the church that the bombs fell in the last air raid on Gosport, a week before D-Day. Four people were killed and an infants' school was reduced to rubble.

An extensive graveyard was once among the key features at Holy Trinity Church.

The graves have been cleared, giving Holy Trinity Church a much more open aspect.

Post-war, the area was redeveloped with flats, including Harbour and Seaward Towers in the early 1960s. With land for housing so limited in the area and with no desire to return to the cramped accommodation which characterised the pre-war years, the obvious answer was to build skywards – all of which gives the area around the church a much-altered aspect.

Gone too is the graveyard clearly visible in this older image of Holy Trinity Church. The 1911 *Pocket Guide to Gosport* notes 'The extensive graveyard adjoining the church contains many memorials, one or two of which are of a more than passing interest'. Sadly the interest did indeed pass when the graveyard was cleared. Holy Trinity consequently now enjoys a much more open setting than it ever did before.

'A Chaste And Handsome Edifice'

For the first century and a half of its existence, Holy Trinity was 'within the Parish and the Liberties of the Parish Church of Alverstoke', a chapelry of St Mary's. It became a parish in its own right in 1860.

Inevitably it has seen many changes over the years. The church was barely 30 years old when the first set of repairs was needed, costing £121. Soon after, the portico was added.

Not long afterwards, the church was enlarged at its eastern end, as seen in these photographs. A semi-dome supported on pilasters with intricate Roman detailing was incorporated into the main structure.

The graveyard extended beyond the eastern, harbour end of Gosport's Holy Trinity Church.

Again, the graves have long since been cleared.

More change came in 1830 when the dangerous state of the roof prompted the raising of the side walls, the construction of a new roof and the galleries being brought forward.

The next major change came in 1887 when the church was entirely remodelled and the west end rebuilt. Two years later, it gained its distinctive bell tower. A landmark for naval captains, the campanile was designed by Sir Arthur Blomfield (1829–99).

The fourth son of the Anglican Bishop of London, Blomfield became president of the Architectural Association in 1861 and vice-president of the Royal Institute of British Architects (RIBA) in 1886. Regarded as one of the last great Gothic revivalists, he focused principally on church building and restoration – all of which interested the young Thomas Hardy who worked in his London office in 1862.

Inside, the features of the church are striking. *A Topographical Dictionary Of England* (1848) notes: 'It is now a spacious, and, particularly as regards its internal appearance, a chaste and handsome edifice of the Ionic order'. The Church itself goes further, claiming 'probably the most beautiful interior in the south of England, its white walls and barrel-arch ceiling serving as the perfect foil for the marble of the high altar.'

Perhaps the church's best-known feature is its organ, formerly in the private chapel of the mansion of Canons, belonging to the Duke of Chandos. From 1718–20, Handel was director of music to James Brydges, Duke of Chandos, and there can be little doubt that Handel would have played on the organ which was sold to Holy Trinity for £117 in 1748.

Gosport's Congregational Church was one of the town's wartime casualties.

Lost In The War

The present offers a pretty poor substitute when you look at the church which once stood on the current site of Gosport's main post office.

Here, until it was destroyed by German bombs in 1941, stood the Congregational Church, a grand-looking building which was part of a proud tradition. Built in 1794 on the site of a former theatre, the church was the Chapel of the Dissenters.

The English Dissenters were Christians who separated from the Church of England. Opposed to State interference in religious matters, they started their own communities in the 16th, 17th and 18th centuries.

It is possible that the Dissenters had a chapel in Gosport as early as 1663. It was certainly established well before 1700, but it was in the Congregational Church that the Dissenters found their best expression, thanks in large part to the efforts of a remarkable man – David Bogue.

Bogue, whose name lives on in the David Bogue Hall off Stoke Road, became the minister to the Gosport independent chapel in 1774 and played a key role in the town. He was one of the founders of what became the London Missionary Society, and among the students at the academy for the training of missionaries which he set up in Gosport High Street was David Livingstone.

Bogue's was a tough task. His friend James Bennett – with whom he wrote a four-volume *History of Dissenters* – recorded: 'Gosport contains 5,000 inhabitants and can boast little that is attractive;

for the place has the narrowness and slander of a small country town, without its rural simplicity, and with a full share of the vices of Portsmouth, pulled by the fortunes of sailors and the extravagances of harlots. To these evils are added the petty pride and sectarian bigotry of a fortified town.'

Bogue was battling sin in an era which saw scores of pubs within the narrow confines of Gosport's fortified town centre. But despite the obstacles he secured widespread admiration and a place in history – his supporters would argue – as the architect of the modern missionary movement.

Gosport's main post office seems a poor substitute for the church which once stood here.

Gosport's Little Church was connected with the National Children's Home nearby.

Healthy Miracles In A Former Church

'Welcome to the Miracles Spa!' runs the website. 'We are a ladies only facility – yes exclusively for women, creating spaces where activity and relaxation come together so you can relax in the peace and quiet of our surrounds in complete comfort and get away from the usual hustle and bustle of life.'

Put it like that, and you can see that the Miracles Spa resort offers something not a million miles away from the balm the building once dispensed when it served as a church.

'Many of the original internal features and artefacts of the former church, including stained-glass windows, oak pews and pulpits, have been skilfully integrated into the imaginatively created rooms', the spa boasts – an unusual present use for an unusual past church.

The message on the back of the postcard (on pages 130–131), sent in August 1938 to Mr and Mrs Sharman, Kingsway Road, Evington Park, Leicester, explains all: 'Just a wee card from little Auntie A. Here on holiday with Aunt Lizzie. Very comfortable at Hotel. Weather good but very warm. Worshipped at Church – on other side – connection with National Children's Home. Joan Israely is a nurse at the Home. Hope you are both well. I am able to walk much better. Love Auntie A.'

It is worth noting that Auntie A gave her address as 'Alverstoke, near Gosport' – a designation which would have gone down well with the locals.

More pertinently, as Auntie A rightly says, this was the church to the National Children's Home, a facility which continued into the 1970s. I remember a big fête there opened by one of the *Blue*

Now, the church is home to Miracles Spa.

Peter presenters. The home was also part of the Christmas Day round of visits for the Mayor of Gosport when my father held the office from 1974–76.

And all the accounts suggest that this was a good home, enlightened and kind. It was set up by Thomas Bowman Stephenson, a Wesleyan minister in Lambeth, towards the end of the 19th century. Children in his congregation were 'ragged, shoeless, filthy, their faces pinched with hunger and premature wretchedness.' Determined to do something about it, he opened his first home in 1869 and the home in Alverstoke soon after, believing the countryside and sea air would benefit the children enormously.

9. Portsmouth

Hard Work, Long Hours

To the right in this picture is Portsmouth dockyard, a place which has perhaps shaped Gosport more than any other. It was the growth of the dockyard which prompted the growth of Gosport in the 1800s when Gosport's range of service establishments – particularly stores and victualling –

grew up in support of the Royal Navy. And in the 20th century in particular, it was the influx of dockyard workers which accelerated Gosport's rising population.

With the dockyard hemmed in and little land available for housing around it, Gosport was an obvious option for those looking for somewhere to live – not least because it was cheaper. And so a sea of workers would travel to and fro across the harbour each day, the dockyard key to both Portsmouth's and Gosport's economies.

As you arrive in Portsmouth by ferry, you enjoy a good view of the dockyard. At its peak more than 22,000 men and women worked there.

***Today the dockyard offers an unrivalled collection of historic ships including HMS* Victory, *HMS* Warrior *and the* Mary Rose.**

For a time, the dockyard was the largest industrial complex in the country, a place with very much its own culture. At its peak more than 22,000 men and women worked there.

It was hard work with long hours. My grandfather, a crane driver who gained a long-service medal after more than 30 years working in the dockyard, used to tell the story of how he dozed off on the ferry after a particularly arduous day's work. The ferrymen did not like to disturb him. He had no idea how many times he crossed the harbour before someone finally saw sense and woke him up.

It is a typical story. Find someone with their roots in Gosport, and the chances are that the dockyard will have played a part in their lives.

Today the Historic Dockyard, as the public part is called, offers an unrivalled collection of historic ships including HMS *Victory*, HMS *Warrior* and the *Mary Rose* – in what is marketed as 'the best day out in the south of England.'

Ships from Portsmouth were an important part of the fleet that drove off the Spanish Armada in 1588; four centuries later, there were emotional scenes as ships sailed from Portsmouth to the Falklands, some never to return.

Her Majesty's Naval Base (HMNB) Portsmouth is one of three operating bases for the Royal Navy, alongside HMNB Clyde and HMNB Devonport. Home to the oldest surviving dry dock in the world, it is the base port for two thirds of the Royal Navy's surface fleet.

Pride Of The City

In recent years, The Spinnaker Tower has become something of a symbol for the city of Portsmouth – a modern, highly-attractive tower in a go-ahead part of the city, the beautifully and excitingly designed Gunwharf Quays. But nothing can eclipse HMS *Victory* as Portsmouth's premier icon.

Nelson's flagship at the Battle of Trafalgar, the *Victory* is the only surviving warship that fought in the American War of Independence, the French Revolutionary War and the Napoleonic Wars – a fascinating piece of naval heritage which, if anything, grows more fascinating with every visit.

My grandfather, who worked for so many years in the dockyard, loved to take me and my brother on the *Victory* as boys. He used to joke that we had been on it more times than Nelson. And maybe we had. But with that tarry smell and those beams which only children could pass under unbowed, it was a place you could never tire of.

HMS *Victory* was built in Chatham Dockyard and launched on 7 May 1765. Nelson was standing on the deck of the *Victory* when he was shot and fatally wounded at the Battle of Trafalgar on 21 October 1805. By the time he died, just over three hours later, a great victory had been won.

This lovely older image shows the *Victory* in Portsmouth Harbour at a time when Gosport contributed £75 a year towards the warship's maintenance. Her active career ended in 1812, seven years after the Battle of Trafalgar, when she was moored in Portsmouth Harbour off Gosport and used as a depot ship.

HMS Victory, *Nelson's flagship at the Battle of Trafalgar, deteriorated during her years afloat in Portsmouth Harbour.*

H. M. S. VICTORY, PORTSMOUTH

HMS Victory *was taken into dry dock in the dockyard on 12 January 1922 where work began on restoring her to her 1805 condition.*

For a while, she served as the Naval School of Telegraphy, and insufficient attention was paid to her upkeep. By the early 1920s, she was in a very poor condition. Following a national appeal led by the Society for Nautical Research, she was taken into dry dock in the dockyard on 12 January 1922 where work began on restoring her to her 1805 condition.

Housing The Dockers

Walking up the pier from the ferry, you come to Portsea, the area of Portsmouth which grew up around the dockyard.

When Henry VII founded the dockyard in 1495, it was separated from Portsmouth by fields. The area, known as Portsmouth Common until it became Portsea in 1792, was principally farmland, but as the dockyard grew in size and importance, so the area around it began to be developed. It became almost a new town in its own right, which at one time threatened to outdo Portsmouth both in terms of the beauty of its buildings and the size of its population. In 1801 Portsea was home to 25,000 people, more than

THE COMMON HARD PORTSEA.

Portsea and the area around the dockyard grew rapidly as the dockyard grew in importance.

three times the population of Old Portsmouth. Gradually, however, it merged with the city and stands indistinct from it today.

Portsea's character is well evoked in the *Victoria County History* of 1908: 'The streets are narrow, and the houses for the most part low, with tiled roofs and doors approached by two steps from the street. Some of the lowest houses are still known as garrison houses, because, it is said, the inhabitants were not allowed to build them higher lest they should interfere with the outlook from the old fortifications.'

'Still narrower, ill-paved alleys intersect the town in its poorest parts. The high walls of the dockyard bound it on two sides, while along the third runs the Hard, a roadway leading by the harbour-side to the main gates of the yard.'

By then, the Portsea Extension Railway, as it was known, had connected the town station with the harbour, where a new station was built on a pier in 1876. Facing the harbour is the row of houses seen in the image above – 'chiefly taverns, where the sailors used to be paid off', the 1908 account noted, 'while on the wooden seats opposite watermen wait to take visitors to Nelson's flagship, the *Victory*, or round the harbour.' The area was badly bombed during World War Two and extensively redeveloped in the 1950s and 1960s.

In the late 1970s, the area to the right of the pier was infilled to create a bus terminal hovering over the water, seen in the more recent image. Part of my Saturday job in Gosport 30 years ago

Buses park where boats once moored.

included collecting the weekly sports newspaper *The Sports Mail* every Saturday night from Portsmouth during the football season. Week by week, I watched the pillars grow out of the water and the new bus station slowly emerge.

Rising From The Ruins

A symbol of the city of Portsmouth, the Guildhall embodies both the city's pride and its suffering, its past glories and the way it has rebuilt itself following the devastation of the Blitz.

Designed in the neo-classical style by architect William Hill, it was built at a cost of £140,000 on land which had once been a brewery, after the previous town hall had proved too small for the growing town. The new site was chosen because of its proximity to the railway line, which was becoming increasingly important. On completion, it was opened by the Prince and Princess of Wales (later Edward VII and Queen Alexandra) in 1890, and with Portsmouth's elevation to city status in 1926, the Town Hall was renamed the Guildhall.

Fifteen years later, it was a smouldering shell, gutted by a devastating blaze – the result of some of the incendiary bombs which fell on Portsmouth on the night of 10 January 1941. The building took weeks to cool, but there was no need to get inside it to confirm the sad fact:

Portsmouth Guildhall was opened by the future Edward VII in 1890.

Portsmouth's Guildhall had effectively been destroyed, with just the outer walls – and not all of those – still standing.

After the war, there was a strong argument for demolishing it altogether and starting from scratch. But for many Portsmouth people, demolition would have been to complete the Germans' work. Instead the Guildhall rose again as a symbol of the city's indestructible spirit. The remains were incorporated into the new building which was opened by the Queen on 8 June 1959.

Centrally located, the Guildhall is the biggest events venue in Portsmouth, offering weddings, banquets, conferences, exhibitions, festivals, ceremonies, birthday parties and business meetings. It is also home to a huge range of events including concerts from the biggest names in pop and rock, and visits from the country's leading comedians. In recent years, the Guildhall has also hosted the national final of the Live & Unsigned competition which sets out to find the best unsigned talent in the country.

The Guildhall rose again after the Blitz, though it has sadly lost the open aspect it enjoyed in the earlier image.

Today it looks out across a very different Portsmouth to the one that used to surround it. Its own reflection stares back at it in the glass-fronted Civic Centre buildings designed to complement it.

The Church Without A Roof

It was widely believed among schoolboys in Alverstoke in the 1970s that the tree in the centre of the village was the hanging tree on which criminals had been executed. We also believed – equally erroneously – that Portsmouth's Royal Garrison Church had had its roof neatly whipped off by Gosport's besieging Parliamentarians as they tried to show Royalist Portsmouth just who was the boss. The truth is that it was the German Luftwaffe that did the damage.

A scheduled ancient monument dating back to 1212–20, it originally formed part of the Hospital of St John and St Nicholas (God's House or *Domus Dei*), and was founded as a shelter for pilgrims from overseas heading for the Shrine at Canterbury. The church was closed under Henry VIII and briefly served as an armoury. Once Henry had gone, however, it enjoyed rather more positive royal associations.

Portsmouth's Royal Garrison Church was once a focal point for the armed forces – a role reflected in its wealth of memorials.

Today, the Royal Garrison Church is both ruin and memorial. Nearby, a statue commemorates Vice-Admiral Horatio Nelson (29 September 1758–21 October 1805) whose flagship HMS Victory can be visited in the dockyard.

Charles II married Catherine of Braganza here in 1662, James II visited the church in 1672, and George III and Queen Charlotte attended the Divine Service in 1778. Throughout this time it was used for services for the troops of the garrison.

A measure of the church's distinction is the wealth of memorials to distinguished personages it contains. Indeed, nearly 300 memorials are associated with the church. Among them are Vice-Admiral Horatio Viscount Nelson, Field Marshal Lord Raglan, Admiral Sir Henry Ducie Chads, General Sir Alexander Dickson, Field Marshal Arthur Duke of Wellington, Lt Gen Sir John Moore and Field Marshal Sir Alexander Woodford. Somewhat less to the church's credit is that in 1449 it witnessed the murder of the Bishop of Chichester – which led to Portsmouth being excommunicated for 50 years.

Then, on 10 January 1941, the same night that fire ravaged the Guildhall, flames gutted the nave of the Garrison Church. Assisted by soldiers and airmen, the verger Mr J. Heaton was able to save the chancel, which is still enclosed today. The nave, however, remains roofless – and it is certain to stay that way. English Heritage and the University of Portsmouth have concluded that a roof would probably accelerate the deterioration of the stone. The argument is that over the years the exposed stonework has absorbed considerable amounts of salt solution which would crystallise if the roof were replaced, damaging the walls.

It has consequently been left as a partial ruin – a memorial to all those servicemen who gave their lives for their country.

Seaside Amusements

Elegance is the word that comes to mind as you look at the following gorgeous image of Southsea's Clarence Pier in its heyday. People – not a bare head in sight – are taking the air. Smartly dressed, they really are part of another world. The same scene today simply does not bear comparison.

The glory days of our seaside resorts have long since gone, but at least the pier still stands – credit to Portsmouth when so many others towns have lost theirs, many of which simply crumbled into the sea.

Clarence Pier, which unusually goes along the coast rather than out to sea, is lauded by its owners as the 'largest amusement park on the south coast' boasting 'all manner of amusements, rides and activities for all the family' with 'plenty of food and drink outlets including our 100-seat Wimpy Express fast-food restaurant.'

It would be intriguing to know what the Victorians would make of it today.

The pier was opened in 1861 by the Prince and Princess of Wales and was originally known as Southsea Pier. For the first 12 years of its existence, it was connected by tramline to Portsmouth Town railway station (now Portsmouth & Southsea). From the pier, passengers travelled by steam to the Isle of Wight.

The pier was damaged by air raids during World War Two, and planning permission was granted for its rebuilding in September 1950. By the late 1950s, Clarence Pier had gained its funfair. It opened in its current form in 1961 – an important decade in the pier's development.

Dating back to 1861, Clarence Pier offered refined amusements in a more elegant age.

Southsea.

The amusements continue to this day at Clarence Pier.

The late 1960s brought planning permission for a single-storey amusement arcade on the pier decks, and in the 1990s Clarence Pavilion was converted from a restaurant/ballroom to an amusement arcade with bingo.

Piece by piece, it gained all the essentials of the quintessential seaside entertainment complex – though it was not always terribly PC. I remember in the early 1970s posing for photographs with monkeys on the pier – all part of the seaside fun, though the monkeys probably never saw it that way in their preposterous knitted trouser suits.

More recently, one of its celebrated additions was the futuristic dinosaur-themed ride Jurassic 3001 which lasted from 1994 to 2004. Its best-remembered feature was an animatronic stegosaurus with a protruding head that roared at people passing by.

That Sinking Feeling

Another elegant image, another photograph of a highly-civilised past, complete with reminders of Southsea's important military contribution. Southsea Castle is the perfect backdrop for the servicemen in the foreground.

All is peaceful in both images – a far cry from the horror which must have engulfed the area when Henry VIII's flagship, the *Mary Rose*, tragically sank in front of the castle on 19 July 1545.

Poor design and tidal forces may have been the cause. Others argue she turned too sharply and submerged her open gun ports. These may have been too near to the waterline, and it seems a large number of soldiers in full armour on her upper decks made her even more unstable.

Southsea Castle was built in 1544 and saw tragedy a year later when the **Mary Rose** *sank nearby.*

Southsea Castle is one of the landmarks on Southsea's attractive seafront.

She was first rediscovered in 1836 when a fishing net caught on the wreck, but within a few years she had been forgotten again. The first serious modern search was launched in 1965, and in 1982 she was raised. The surviving section of the ship is now kept in Portsmouth Historic Dockyard where a new museum is currently being built around her.

As for Southsea Castle, it had barely been completed when the *Mary Rose* tragedy struck. Built in haste in 1544, it occupies a key position at the mouth of Portsmouth Harbour and served as one of a series of fortifications constructed by Henry VIII against the ever-looming threat of invasion. Portsmouth was crucial – and Southsea Castle was part of the plan to guard it.

In the early 17th century, the castle fell into disrepair and was damaged by fire. During the English Civil War it was captured by the Parliamentarians, but the castle knew better times soon afterwards when renewed threat of invasion prompted Charles II to repair and improve it.

In the 19th century, the castle was used as a military prison – though its guns remained ready for action. After more than five centuries of service, the castle was bought by Portsmouth City Council in 1960 and returned to its 19th-century appearance. It opened to the public in 1967.

The Rise Of The Resort

Portsmouth's seaside resort is Southsea. Though it lies within the boundary of Portsmouth borough, it has a style all its own – one which has faded only slightly from Britain's beach holiday heyday. The open spaces, a largely undeveloped shoreline and the many attractive residences which face the sea make Southsea an attractive place to stroll.

Southsea's rise as a seaside resort meant new hotels were needed. The Queen's Hotel was rebuilt in 1903 following a fire which gutted the original building.

The Queen's Hotel on Clarence Parade is one of Southsea's many fine buildings.

Southsea came into favour as a seaside resort during the Peninsular War and continued to develop throughout the 1800s. Among the many striking buildings is the Queen's Hotel, which was originally built by the architect Augustus Livesay in 1861. Known as Southsea House, it was a private home owned by Sir John and Lady Morris, surrounded by woods and enjoying, as it does today, superb views towards the Solent and the Isle of Wight.

When it was rented to William Kemp Jnr, it became one of the first hotels in Southsea, but disaster struck as the century closed. The building was gutted by a devastating fire on 8 December 1891. The hotel was rebuilt in 1903 by the architect T.W. Cutler as the impressive building that stands today, complete with its Edwardian baroque style in brown terracotta.

Both Livesay and Cutler were important architects of their day. Livesay is the man behind St Mary's Church in Andover, a design regarded as a fine example of Early Victorian Gothic. In Portsmouth, he was the architect of Holy Trinity Church, the last remains of which can be seen in the grounds of Trinity House, Anchor Gate Road. The church, requested by the dockyard workers, was built between 1837–41 at the end of North Street, Portsea, 'it having been represented to the Ordnance Office that another place of worship was needed by men in Government Employment.'

The foundation stone was laid on 20 June 1839, and the building was completed of local flint and Portland stone at a total cost of £3,300 to serve a district of 7,000 people. It was destroyed by bombs in 1941 and deconsecrated after the war.

Thomas William Cutler (1842–1909) was an architect known particularly for his work in designing cottages and country buildings. He studied at King's College, the Royal Academy Schools and the South Kensington Schools. Among his other works are houses and studios in Abbey Place, St John's Wood, London.

A Green Space For Every Occasion

It is a delight to wander along the sea front at Southsea, but just as appealing is to relax on Southsea Common, a haven for ball games, kite-flying, picnicking or simply unwinding.

A substantial open space bought from the War Department in 1922, Southsea Common has long been a place where people come together. Thousands gathered there to watch Portsmouth's 2008 FA Cup triumph on a vast TV screen, and the Common was lined with thousands more the following day when manager Harry Redknapp and his players brought the cup back to Portsmouth for the first time since 1939.

Southsea Common also had a key role to play in the D-Day 50 commemorations held in June 1994 to mark the 50th anniversary of D-Day, and it was to Southsea Common again that Portsmouth turned for Trafalgar 200, a programme marking 200 years since the Battle of Trafalgar, the encounter in which Nelson was fatally wounded. The commemoration culminated in a firework display claimed to be largest the UK has ever seen.

Both events harked back to Southsea Common's important military role. It was here that armies gathered before going to war, as far back as the Battle of Crécy in 1346.

Appropriately, the Common is now home to Portsmouth's war memorial commemorating officers, ranks and ratings of the port who died at sea during the wars 1914–18 and 1939–45. Part of the inscription reads: 'Of the 24,588 men and women whose names are on this monument 9,666 died during the First World War and 14,922 including 75 from Newfoundland who served in the Royal Navy during the Second World War. All were buried at sea or were otherwise denied by the fortunes of war, a known and honoured grave.'

Southsea Common has long been a place where people gathered.

Southsea Common

D-Day and Trafalgar commemorations are among the events to have been staged on Southsea Common in recent times.

Few were the families in the area who were not touched by the wars. Among the names is my great-uncle Bob Millener. He survived the sinking of HMS *Barham* on 25 November 1941 and was highly amused when my mother, just a child, accidentally bloodied his nose – something the Germans had not managed to do. He perished in the sinking of HMS *Quorn* on 3 August 1944.

On a lighter note, on the corner of Castle Road and Southsea Terrace facing Southsea Common, a blue plaque marks the birthplace of the comedian Peter Sellers.

Guarding The Harbour Entrance

The Round Tower in Old Portsmouth is another part of the city's centuries-old fortifications and dates from the early 15th century.

In 1415, Henry V carried out the first fleet review at Spithead before sailing to war against the French. Fortifying Portsmouth became vital, and he ordered the construction of the Round Tower in 1418. Built in wood, it was completed in 1426, and the Square Tower nearby was added in 1494, the year before the dockyard was established.

Henry VIII ordered the Round Tower to be rebuilt in stone, strengthening the fortifications considerably. A Tudor account describing 'the este side of Portesmuth Haven' notes 'there is at this point of the haven Portesmuth toun, and a great round tourre almost doble in quantite and strenkith to that that is on the west side of the haven right agayn it: and heere is a might(y) chaine of yren to draw from tourre to towrre.'

Portsmouth's Round Tower guards the harbour entrance in this image, a postcard sent in 1907.

Gosport's skyline has changed considerably in the century since the earlier photograph was taken.

Defences continued to be added until the mid-19th century.

The tower has long been a key place from which to watch the ships entering or leaving the port, and the view would have been a particularly striking one in June 1944 as D-Day approached. Portsmouth was at the centre of the preparations, a story well told in the city's D-Day Museum. The water in front of the Round Tower and off Clarence Pier was filled with warships waiting for the signal to invade.

The top of the Round Tower remains open to this day and is still a great place from which to enjoy the harbour, helped by a plaque which identifies the various points in the panoramic view.

In recent years, the area has attracted a number of pursuits, some good, some not so good. Artists display their works most attractively on the land side of the fortifications. Meanwhile, on the sea side, there are occasional outbreaks of the craze grimly known as 'tomb-stoning'. Youngsters risk all by jumping at height into the water – a practice met with justifiable disapproval.

10. Final Thoughts

As part of the winding down of the Royal Naval Hospital at Haslar in March 2007, the last commanding officer, Surgeon Captain James Campbell, led a parade from the gates of Haslar Hospital over Haslar Bridge to the Millennium Promenade. With its ceremony and colour, its turn-out and pageantry, it was an event which truly marked the end of an era. This book has been about the changes which have brought us to this point.

In these pages, I have outlined Gosport's expansion from an insignificant fishing village to become a key base for a wide range of military and naval services. I have also looked at the post-war retraction, of which the closure at Haslar is the latest example.

Barracks are barracks no more; the submarines have gone; and so too now has Gosport's huge naval hospital – all services around which Gosport grew.

The early years of the 21st century see a proud naval town entering a new chapter in its history. Gone are the days when up to a third of the peninsula's land area was in the hands of the Ministry of Defence. In the next few decades we will see whether the departing services have left behind them a void or an opportunity. Gosport is redefining itself even as we watch.

Postcards are snapshots of a moment, and my father's substantial collection offers rich possibilities – an ideal way to look back at a Gosport which has changed forever. As a measure of that change, I have replicated some of his postcards to show how the sites and sights look now.

It has been a fascinating task, and one which is not simply about wallowing in the past. Nor has it been simply about navel (or perhaps naval) gazing in the present. Put past and present together and you start to beg questions about the future.

Many of the postcards featured in this book date from the first 30 years of the 20th century. My present-day photographs are the equivalent postcards of the early 21st century. How will those postcards look at the start of the 22nd century?

The only certainty is that the pace of change will continue to accelerate. The changes between 1909 and 2009 have been baffling and bewildering; we cannot even begin to imagine what will happen between 2009 and 2109.

But, with Gosport in transition, it is worth remembering that much of the change has been for the better. Gosport's slums have been cleared; poor sanitation has long since been banished; and the quality of the town's accommodation has improved considerably.

Even before World War Two had ended, Gosport was planning its post-war housing provision. It has always been a forward-thinking borough – the product of increasingly enlightened times.

One final card before finishing. My father's favourite – and mine too – among the messages on the backs of the postcards in his collection is one written exactly 100 years ago. It is, thankfully, unimaginable now.

An image of Portsmouth Harbour from exactly a century ago.

Not the friendliest or politest of messages.

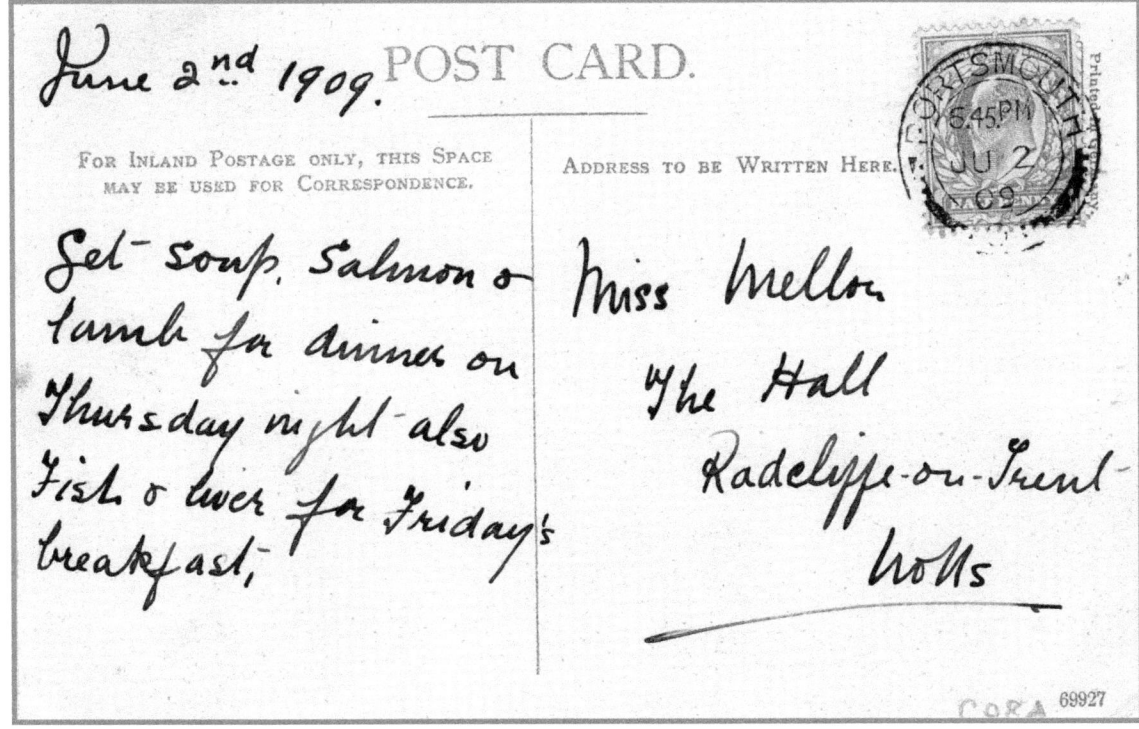

Showing the view from Gosport towards Portsmouth, it was written on 2 June 1909 to Miss Mellor at The Hall, Radcliffe-on-Trent, Notts. It says simply: 'Get soup, salmon & lamb for dinner on Thursday night. Also fish and liver for Friday's breakfast.'

No 'please', no 'thank you', no name, no signature. No 'Dear Miss Mellor', no 'best wishes'. I find it difficult enough to imagine anyone consuming fish and liver for breakfast nowadays; it is even more difficult to imagine anyone speaking to anyone else like that now.

The message shows – as much as any image in this book – just how far we have come in the 100 years since 1909. The message is priceless. And so too is the town in which it was written.

Roll of Honour

Councillor Roger P. Allen

Penny Bennett

Ted and Audrey Brett

Dave Brindley

Joyce Brown

Lesley Burton

Michael Carr

Mr & Mrs A.P. Chubb

Anne Cooper

June and Shaun Cully

Kathleen Cummings née Pit

Rob Diamond

Geoff Evans

Gordon and Yvonne Flory

Chris Giffen

Richard Giffen

Corinne Goodwin

Liz and Ted Goodyer

Robert Gower

Roy Harris

Caroline and Ian Hawkes

Graham and Juliette Hewitt

Councillor Rob Hylands

Mr & Mrs Kilsby

Councillor Derek Kimber

Adrian Knight

Pat Lee née Nicholson

Mr George Lewis

Joan Lockhart

Mick Mears

Maureen and David Miles

Peggy Radford

Tim Ricketts

David Rogers

Brian John Russell

Mr A.G. Scott

Miss J. Seymour

Mr B. Simmons

Linda Smart

Alfred Steel

Lesley Stubbings

Mrs Maureen Swire

Sally Taylor

Peter Tobin

Evelyn Upfold

Jean and George Watson

Ray Whitehead

Dave Whymark

Pamela Wrenn

Dennis Wright

)

BV - #0058 - 280426 - C0 - 276/195/7 - PB - 9781780913902 - Gloss Lamination